Jimmy Carter

GREAT LIFE STORIES

Jimmy Carter

PRESIDENT AND PEACEMAKER

DAVID SEIDMAN

FRANKLIN WATTS
A Division of Scholastic Inc.
New York Toronto London Auckland Sydney
Mexico City New Delhi Hong Kong
Danbury, Connecticut

To Richard Howell, who understands what it is like to be a leader

ACKNOWLEDGMENTS

Editor Wendy Mead hired me to write this book and proved amazingly patient when I ran late. Of everyone who helped me with this book, she is the most important.

My research assistants were indispensable. The one who contributed the most was the amazing Lael Welch, but others provided documents and help in getting this book organized: Dawn Shannon, Allison Littleton, Helen Kim, and Kate Coe.

Thanks to all.

Photographs © 2004: AP/Wide World Photos: 24 (A.A. Bradley), 66 (Wilson), 15, 32; Archive Photos/Getty Images: 10, 27, 47; Corbis Images: 2, 33, 39, 43, 50, 59, 76, 82 (Bettmann), 35, 86 (Kevin Fleming), 57 (Owen Franken), 16, 18 (Raymond Gehman), 92 (Robert Maass), 52, 63 (Wally McNamee), 87 (Mathew Mendelsohn), 105 (Les Stone), cover (Mike Theiler/Reuters NewMedia Inc.), 6, 44, 79 (UPI), 13, 28, 64, 74, 75, 88, 96; Corbis Sygma/Gilbert Liz: 99; Getty Images: cover (David Hume Kennerly), 61 (Kean Collection), 111 (Arne Knudsen); Jimmy Carter Library: 9, 12, 41, 45, 72; Roger Miller Photo, Ltd.: 22; The Carter Center/Rick Diamond: 108.

Library of Congress Cataloging-in-Publication Data

Seidman, David.
  Jimmy Carter : president and peacemaker / David Seidman.
    p. cm. — (Great life stories)
  Includes bibliographical references and index.
  ISBN 0-531-12374-X
  1. Carter, Jimmy, 1924—Juvenile literature. 2. Presidents—United States—Biography—Juvenile literature.
I. Title. II. Series.

E873.S44 2004
973.918'092—dc22

                                                                    2004007169

Contents

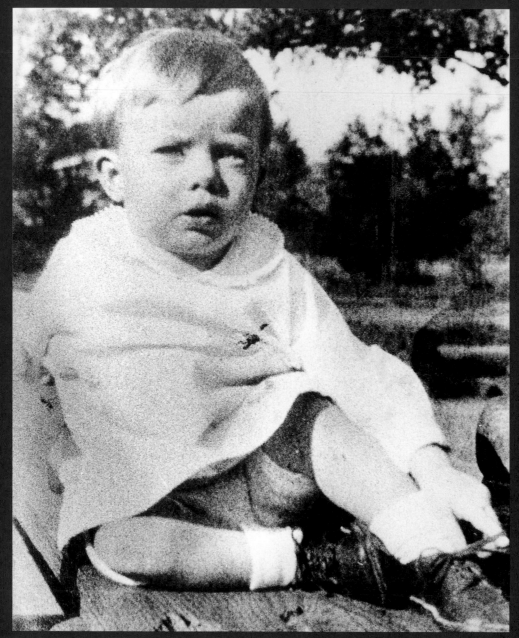

Jimmy Carter was born and raised in rural Georgia.

ONE

Family Business

James Earl Carter, Jr., known as "Jimmy," was born in rural Georgia. While he focused on life on the farm in his early days, this small-town boy would grow up to become the thirty-ninth president of the United States. He sought to bring faith and trust into government and to improve international relations, particularily in the Middle East.

Since leaving office, Jimmy has been an activist and advocate, traveling the world to talk leaders into peacefully resolving political and social conflicts. In 2002, he won the Nobel Peace Prize for his efforts. Despite all of his accomplishments, he has never forgotten where he came from and has maintained strong ties to the tiny community of Plains, Georgia.

GEORGIA ROOTS

One of Jimmy's ancestors, Thomas Carter, moved from England to Virginia's Isle of Wight County in 1637 when he was twenty-five. Thomas's descendants moved throughout Virginia, North Carolina, and Georgia. Virtually every generation settled new land until 1851, when Thomas's great-great-grandson Wiley settled in what is now southwest Georgia's Sumter County. Wiley planted a farm on land that other Carters, including Jimmy, would still plow more than a century later.

Around 1840, about 20 miles (32 kilometers) from Wiley's farm, some settlers had established a new community. It stood on plains so flat that "when it rained, the rain just stayed there. It didn't know which way to run," Jimmy Carter said in 2001. The settlers named it the Plains of Dura, after a spot mentioned in the Bible's Book of Daniel. After 1885, the citizens shortened the name to the simpler Plains, and Carters would live in the area for decades.

World War I

Though the United States only entered the war in 1917, World War I had actually started three years earlier. Sparked in part by the assassination of Archduke Franz Ferdinand of Austria-Hungary, the war was a conflict in which France, Britain, and Russia fought together against Austria-Hungary, Germany, and Italy. The United States stayed out of the war until German submarines started sinking American ships. The U.S. Congress declared war on Germany on April 6, 1917.

EARL CARTER

On September 12, 1894, Wiley Carter's great-grandson James Earl Carter was born. Like many other southerners, he stopped using his first name, and people simply called him Earl. He attended Riverside Military Academy, an all-male boarding school about 160 miles (260 km) north of Plains, and fought in World War I. These experiences may have taught him the hard discipline that he later imposed on his son Jimmy.

After the war ended in 1918, Earl returned to Plains and opened a general store. Always looking for ways to earn extra money, he bought fields to farm and other properties to sell or rent. By the beginning of 1920, he was twenty-six years old, and Sumter County's young women were noticing him.

JIMMY'S MOTHER, LILLIAN

In 1920, Bessie Lillian Gordy was twenty-two years old and a student at Plains's Wise Sanitarium, a hospital and school for nurses. Like Earl, she had dropped her first name and became known simply as Lillian.

Jimmy's father, Earl Carter, was an enterprising, strong man.

Lillian and Earl Carter met after Earl returned from serving in World War I.

At least two stories tell how she met Earl. One has him spotting her at a dance. Another has Samuel Wise, one of Lillian's teachers and a founder of her school, noticing the rising young businessman and introducing him to Lillian. In any event, the two strong-willed, lively, sharply intelligent Georgians were soon dating.

Lillian had grown up in Richland, less than 20 miles (30 km) from Plains. Her father, James Jackson Gordy, became Richland's postmaster and grew active in politics, campaigning for candidates in election after election. Unlike most white southerners, Gordy spent at least part of his political career working to unite the races. His daughter became one of the few white people in the area to treat blacks as equals, a behavior that she passed on to her son.

ENTER JIMMY

On September 26, 1923, Earl and Lillian married. On October 1, 1924, Lillian gave birth to James Earl Carter, Jr. in the facility where she had

The Segregated South

Racial segregation, or the practice of keeping people of different races apart, was widespread in the south while Jimmy Carter was growing up. African Americans were treated poorly and were forced to use separate facilities from whites, such as schools and water fountains. They were also forced to sit in separate sections of vehicles, restaurants, movie theaters, and other places.

Jimmy was the Carters' first child, but more would follow.

studied nursing. They brought him home to a small house with no running water or electricity. Kerosene lamps provided light but filled the air with a smoky, oily smell. Water came from a well in the yard, and Jimmy later remembered lugging heavy buckets of water into the kitchen. There was no toilet. Inside the house, the Carters used a simple pot, and outside they used a privy. A privy is a small building housing a bench that had a hole over a pit. This setup was normal for a middle-class family living in southwestern Georgia at the time.

Next door lived another young family. Wilburn Edgar Smith and his wife Allie Murray Smith had a daughter named Rosalynn, who was born on August 18, 1927. Jimmy didn't know it, but he was going to marry her.

On October 22, 1926, Jimmy's sister Gloria was born. Earl realized that his growing family would overcrowd their little house. In 1928, he moved them to a farmhouse in Archery, a town west of Plains. The extra space came in handy. On August 7, 1929, Lillian gave birth to another daughter, Ruth.

FARM LIFE

Archery wasn't quite a town. It was a collection of people, land, and buildings with no mayor or city council. Government was the Sumter County seat in Americus, more than 10 miles (16 km) to the east. As for the Carters' home, Jimmy said in 2001, "Life on the farm then was much more like it was in the time of Moses or Jesus than it is today." Like most southern farmers, Earl owned no tractors or other machinery.

The Carters planted primarily cotton and peanuts. They also raised watermelon, corn, potatoes, and other crops, as well as pigs and other livestock. They raised some of the animals as meat for Earl to sell in a small store that he built on the property.

Like the house in Plains, the Archery home had no electricity. For heat, the Carters burned logs in a stove or fireplace. Jimmy's bedroom

When Jimmy's sister, Gloria, was born, the family decided to move to a farm in Archery, Georgia.

stood relatively far from the nearest fireplace and was very cold in the winter.

Still, the family did enjoy a few luxuries. With hundreds of acres of land, Earl was one of Archery's more prosperous citizens. An expert tennis player, he built a clay court near the house. The family had a battery-operated radio, a rarity at that time and place, and Jimmy loved to listen to the broadcasts.

Jimmy also loved the outdoors and spent as much time there as he could. Rachel Clark, his nanny and an expert angler, taught him to fish, and he spent many peaceful afternoons by a creek with friends. Even a simple walk could bring him pleasure. Jimmy loved feeling grass under his feet and mud between his toes and never wore shoes while the weather stayed warm.

JIMMY, EARL, AND LILLIAN

The most important person in Jimmy's life was his father. Jimmy idolized the man. Earl worked hard, planned his actions carefully, saved every cent, and watched intently for anything that might improve his businesses. He was relentlessly honest, a trait that his son would adopt.

Earl also could be stern, harsh, and cold. "I hungered for some demonstration of my father's love," Jimmy later recalled. When Earl gave him chores to do around the farm, Jimmy did them eagerly. To the boy's frustration, Earl rarely praised or thanked him. This relationship may have helped the future president develop both sympathy for the oppressed and a willingness to work with tyrants. "He showed his love for me by letting me do things other boys didn't, [like] taking me on hunting trips with his friends," Jimmy remembered.

Earl dominated his family, including the high-spirited Lillian, but he didn't stop her from pursuing her own interests. While most wives of traditional men like Earl stayed home to cook, clean, and raise children, Lillian kept her job as a nurse and sometimes put in twenty-hour workdays. When she wasn't at the hospital in Plains, she checked on the residents of Archery and helped them through illnesses.

WAYS OF LIFE

Because Lillian and Earl weren't home during the day, Jimmy spent his time with his neighbors. Almost all of them were African American, including Alonzo "A. D." Davis, whom the grown-up Jimmy called "the closest friend I've ever had." The boys did everything together.

Jimmy admired, respected, and even loved A. D. and his other African American neighbors but never questioned the racism that constantly afflicted their lives. The boys sometimes caught the Seaboard Airline

To Jimmy, Gloria, and Ruth, their father was a commanding presence in their lives.

Much of life in Plains revolved around the Plains Baptist Church.

Railroad to Americus to see a movie. Jimmy and A. D. had to sit in different cars of the train and different sections of the theater.

Another powerful force in Plains was religion. As Lillian once claimed, "The church is the center of everything in a small town." In 1935, Reverend Royall Callaway of Plains Baptist Church baptized Jimmy, who was "born again." The phrase comes from the Bible's Book of John: "[Jesus said,] 'Unless a man be born again, he cannot see the kingdom of God.'" When asked how someone already born can be born again, Jesus explained, "That which is born of the flesh is flesh, but that which is born of the Spirit [of God] is spirit." In other words, according to Carter's religion, an ordinary birth that brings a body into the world isn't enough. To reach heaven, a person must have a rebirth of his spirit by dedicating himself or herself to God and Jesus.

Earl Carter taught at Plains Baptist's Sunday school, but he spent most of his waking hours making a living, and he wanted his firstborn child to learn how as well. At age five, Jimmy was picking peanuts and selling them to anyone who passed by. In 1933, before he turned nine, he had earned enough cash to start investing.

Cotton was selling at some of the lowest prices in years. Jimmy bought a few bales and tucked them into a shed on the farm. He sold them a few years later, when prices had gone up again. He made enough money from the sale to buy four or five little shacks where poor blacks lived, and he became a teenage landlord.

Making money wasn't his main goal, though. His uncle Tom Watson Gordy had joined the navy, and his postcards from far-off ports fascinated the boy. By age eight, he was yearning to attend the United States Naval Academy (USNA) in Annapolis, Maryland.

USNA candidates had to excel in athletics and scholarship, demonstrate high moral character, and receive a nomination from a senator, congressman, or other high government official. Jimmy could meet the first qualifications on his own, but how could a kid from a small town impress a senator?

Fortunately, Earl was getting involved in politics. He joined the Sumter County school board, supported candidates for election, and took Jimmy to political rallies, giving the future president the first taste of his future career.

Lillian helped Jimmy prepare for the USNA academically by sharing with him a love of reading. The skill came in handy after autumn 1930, when he started elementary school. Georgia had one of the nation's worst educational systems. Fortunately, Jimmy fell under the influence of teacher Julia Coleman. Miss Julia, as Jimmy called her, insisted that her students meet the highest standards.

School forced another change on Jimmy's life. Blacks and whites went to different schools, separating Jimmy from A. D. Davis. For the first time, Jimmy made friends who weren't black.

BILLY AND ROSALYNN

On March 29, 1937, Lillian gave birth to William Alton Carter, nicknamed Billy. Because he was thirteen years older than Billy, Jimmy didn't have much in common with him.

In autumn 1940, Jimmy's former neighbor, Rosalynn Smith, lost her father to leukemia, a form of blood cancer. At the age of thirteen, Rosalynn had to help raise the family's three younger children. She became a serious, compassionate young woman with considerable natural intelligence and practical common sense. She was becoming a suitable mate for a striving boy such as Jimmy, even though the teenagers

Jimmy and Rosalynn both attended Plains High School but did not date each other until years later.

didn't realize it. Jimmy started his senior year at Plains High School in the autumn of 1940 and didn't pay Rosalynn much attention. As he laughingly remembered years later, "I wasn't interested in children like her!"

DISAPPOINTMENT

As 1940 turned into 1941, Earl petitioned the Carters' congressman, Stephen Pace, to recommend Jimmy for admission to the USNA. The teenager seemed like a strong candidate. He had the highest grades in Plains High's senior class, played on the school's basketball team, showed initiative at making money, and usually stayed out of trouble.

Unfortunately, World War II was flaring up. The United States seemed likely to join the fight, and plenty of patriotic young men wanted to enter the naval academy. Possibly because of the large number of applicants, Congressman Pace nominated someone other than Jimmy.

Instead of USNA in Annapolis, the disappointed teenager attended Georgia Southwestern College in Americus. Though the campus lay only 16 miles (28 km) by car from Archery, Jimmy moved into a dormitory there.

Congressman Pace had told Jimmy to wait a year before applying to the naval academy again. Jimmy studied hard and even made the college basketball team, although at 5 feet 9 inches (1.75 meters) he was the squad's shortest man.

In the summer of 1942, the naval academy finally accepted Jimmy. Nevertheless, he would have to wait yet another year before enrolling. No one knows the exact reason why. The academy may simply have had too many applicants in line ahead of him. Besides, the navy depended on high-tech ships and other equipment, and at least one biographer has said that the academy wanted Jimmy to get training in science that Georgia Southwestern didn't offer.

Georgia Tech did, though. The Georgia School of Technology had been training scientists and engineers since the 1880s. It is located in Atlanta, the state's capital and biggest city, about 130 miles (310 km) north of the Americus-Plains-Archery area. Jimmy had rarely seen such a fast-paced place. However, he didn't let the town distract him. "Georgia Tech was the best school in the nation to prepare me for the Naval Academy," he said decades later. "Tech was much more difficult academically than I thought it would be. I've been to four universities, and Tech was the most difficult."

Making life even harder on himself, Jimmy joined the campus's Naval Reserve Officers Training Corps (NROTC). In addition to Georgia Tech's heavy workload, NROTC members took classes in subjects that

Attack on Pearl Harbor

On December 7, 1941, Japan's air force attacked the U.S. naval base in Pearl Harbor, Hawaii. This horrible attack killed more than two thousand soldiers stationed there and destroyed numerous U.S. ships and aircraft. President Franklin D. Roosevelt said that the day of the attack was "a date which will live in infamy." Shortly after the attack, the United States entered World War II.

the navy wanted future officers to master, from world geography to the physics of weaponry. It also demanded hard physical training, rigid obedience to authority, and other military practices.

In June 1943, after Georgia Tech's school year ended, Jimmy boarded a train heading north. At age eighteen, he was on his way to Annapolis to enter the naval academy.

Today, about 4,600 students attend the United States Naval Academy in Annapolis, Maryland.

TWO

Navy Days

The naval academy calls all students midshipmen, but has a special name for first-year students: plebes, from the Latin word *plebs*, which means "common people" or "lower classes." Upperclassmen called them far worse names. They ordered the first-year students to do calisthenics instead of sleep and pounded them with broom handles. "We never ate a peaceful meal," Jimmy Carter said in a speech at the USNA Alumni Association. "There were constant questions, research, songs, poems, reports on obscure athletic events, and recitations [to handle]."

Amid the hazing, plebes had schoolwork to do. The academy trained them in leadership and shipboard life, as well as provided classes in sciences, especially engineering, and humanities such as history and English. The academy regimented every moment and action, even requiring students to march to classes in strict formation.

With World War II grabbing every qualified man, the academy compressed its usual four years of study into three, pushing students even harder than usual. Many plebes dropped out, but not Midshipman Carter. His father had taught him to handle discipline, while Julia Coleman and Georgia Tech had accustomed him to studying. To handle the hazing from upperclassmen, he tried to see it as one challenge at a time, not as ongoing and unending.

During their second year the academy sent midshipmen onto ships to perform actual military duty. The school stationed Carter on the USS *New York*, a ramshackle battleship more than thirty years old that patrolled the East Coast. Carter shouldered tasks from manning an anti-aircraft cannon to polishing decks with holystone, a rough, white rock.

Rosalynn developed a crush on Jimmy Carter once she saw him in his uniform.

THE GIRL BACK HOME

In military terms, "leave" means time off. The USNA gave midshipmen leaves a few times each year. When he could, Carter used them to go home. At least one person there was particularly anxious to see him.

In the summer of 1945, Rosalynn Smith turned eighteen and had just completed her freshman year at Georgia Southwestern College. She had become a beautiful young woman with fair skin and dark hair.

Rosalynn had befriended Ruth Carter and spent a lot of time looking at a photo of Ruth's blue-eyed older brother, who displayed a brilliant-white smile to match his white navy uniform. When Carter came home on summer leave, Rosalynn hoped that he'd notice her, but she was too shy to say much to him.

Toward the end of his leave, Carter finally asked Rosalynn out to a movie. Neither of them has publicly detailed what they did on that date. The next morning, however, when Lillian asked her son how he'd enjoyed going out with Rosalynn, he answered, "She's the girl I want to marry." After he returned to Annapolis, Carter and Rosalynn wrote each other many letters. They spent time together whenever he was home on leave.

In August 1945, while Carter was on a training cruise, President Harry Truman announced that American aircraft had dropped two bombs of a new type on Japan. The two atomic bombs unleashed nuclear energy, the force that powers the sun. Each bomb destroyed an entire city. Together, they forced the Japanese to surrender. Because Japan's allies had already given up, the announcement meant that World War II was over.

MARRIAGE AND CAREER

On June 5, 1946, Rosalynn and the Carters went to Annapolis to watch Carter receive a Bachelor of Science degree. His grades and other achievements ranked him as the sixtieth-best student out of a graduating class of 820, an excellent position. Lillian and Rosalynn pinned bars on his shoulders to designate him Ensign Carter, a naval officer. He then asked Rosalynn to be his wife.

On July 7, they got married in Plains Methodist Church, where Rosalynn worshipped. After a honeymoon, they arrived at the Naval Operating Base at Norfolk, Virginia. The navy had assigned Carter to one of the base's ships, the USS *Wyoming*. Even older than the *New York*, the *Wyoming* had become a floating workshop and testing

The Atomic Bomb

During World War II, U.S. scientists were under a lot of pressure to create an atomic bomb, a type of explosive device that gets its power from a nuclear reaction. The United States hoped to be the first country to create an atomic bomb. They knew that the Germans were also working on building such a weapon. The United States achieved success and discovered just how powerful their new weapon was when it was used in the bombing of the Japanese cities of Hiroshima and Nagasaki. The bombs killed more than 100,000 people in Hiroshima and more than 70,000 people in Nagasaki.

ground for new communications, weapons-control, navigation, and radar systems.

Carter spent most of his time aboard ship, while Rosalynn kept a tiny apartment. Like his father, Carter dominated the household. "I thought I was superior to Rosalynn in every way," he said in 1997. "She was just a young girl from Plains, Georgia. I was kind of a man of the world."

Like other young officers, Carter didn't make much money, and his wife didn't have a paying job. Still, they did treat themselves occasionally. In autumn 1946, "I was assigned to Philadelphia to learn about pending new radar equipment, and one night we decided to splurge and went out to an actual restaurant," he recalled in 2001. "That night we decided to have our first child." Rosalynn gave birth to John William Carter on

Jimmy and Rosalynn Carter got married on July 7, 1946. They are shown here leaving their wedding reception in Plains.

July 3, 1947, in the Portsmouth Naval Hospital near Norfolk. His parents nicknamed him Jack.

The navy kept Carter too busy to do much fathering. It put the aging *Wyoming* out of service on July 23 and assigned its sailors to another old

Carter poses with the rest of the crew aboard the USS *Wyoming*.

ship, the USS *Mississippi*. Carter continued to work on new electronics systems and served as a training and education officer, teaching other sailors how to do their jobs.

The *Mississippi's* captain "exercised his authority in an arbitrary and vindictive way," Carter wrote in his book *Living Faith*. "Life under this commander quickly eroded my sense of commitment to naval service." Carter wanted out. Submarines looked like a promising part of the navy's future, so he applied to submarine school.

He got in. During July 1948, the Carters moved to New London, Connecticut, more than 350 miles (560 km) north of Norfolk and

Integration Underwater

Blacks, whites, and other races didn't mix in the U.S. military at that time. Commanders assigned different races to different units, often refused to promote non-whites, and committed other acts of racism.

The situation started changing after July 26, 1948, when President Truman issued Executive Order 9981. "Establishing the President's Committee on Equality of Treatment and Opportunity in the Armed Services" decreed "equality of treatment and opportunity for all persons in the armed services without regard to race, color, religion, or national origin."

At the time, Carter was aboard a submarine on a training cruise. "It was an evolving experience for me as it was for all Americans, the acknowledgment that racial discrimination was first of all wrong and secondly could be changed legally," Carter said in 2001.

nearly 1,000 miles (1,600 km) by land from Plains, so that Carter could study submarines.

Submarine school ended in December 1948. Between Christmas and New Year's Eve, Carter reported to Hawaii's Pearl Harbor. In the water sat his next assignment, the submarine USS *Pomfret*. Unlike the *New York*, *Wyoming*, and *Mississippi*, the *Pomfret* was less than a decade old and in good shape.

Pomfret fish swim in the Pacific Ocean. So did Carter's submarine. Within a few days of his arrival, the *Pomfret* began a cruise to Asia that separated him from Rosalynn for more than three months. Storms at sea made Carter seasick, but he never tried to slack off from his duties. By that point, he wanted to become chief of naval operations, the navy's highest ranking officer. He refused to risk his chances by showing fear, laziness, or weakness.

When he returned to Pearl Harbor in the spring of 1949, Carter embarked on the happiest months of his military life. On June 5, the navy promoted him to lieutenant, junior grade. When he wasn't at sea, he had time to relax with his family under the warm Hawaiian sun.

Things got even happier on April 12, 1950, when Rosalynn gave birth to James Earl Carter III at Honolulu's Tripler Army Medical Center. The nurses felt that the baby looked like his father and dubbed him "a chip off the old block." From then on, the Carters called their son Chip.

Their joy ended when the Korean War began. After World War II, the United States and Soviet Union had divided the Asian nation of Korea. U.S. troops protected South Korea, while the Soviets oversaw North Korea. The Soviets wanted North Korea's government and economy to be communist, much like their own. When North Korean troops invaded the South in June 1952, the United States found itself at war.

Carter wanted to go to Korea. He had trained for war and needed combat experience to qualify for the navy's highest ranks. Instead, the navy ordered the *Pomfret* to San Diego, California. Apparently, navy authorities had judged the ship unready for full-scale war.

The Carters found San Diego crowded and less appealing than Hawaii, but they weren't there for long. After a few months, Carter got orders to report back to New London. The navy wanted him to oversee the final construction and testing of *K-1*, an advanced submarine.

Carter enjoyed the high-tech work and hoped to command *K-1* when it went into service. Not long after he started work, though, Hyman Rickover entered his life. As Carter said decades later, "Second

Communism and the Soviet Union

Communism is a theory that calls for all property to be owned by the community rather than by individuals. In Russia, rebels called Bolsheviks overthrew the ruling royal family in 1917 and established their own form of communist government. Under the new government, the Communist Party ran the country and owned all the businesses and most of the farms. The country and the formerly independent nations that it controlled became known as the Union of Soviet Socialist Republics, also called the Soviet Union.

to my own father, Admiral Rickover had more effect on my life than any other man."

WORKING WITH ADMIRAL RICKOVER

Known as persistent and a perfectionist, Admiral Hyman Rickover was both honored and hated. The grumpy, tireless man also had a visionary streak. Navy submarines ran on diesel fuel, a form of oil. Rickover wanted to run submarines on nuclear energy. In 1950, President Truman ordered the navy to build the *Nautilus* and the *Seawolf*, America's first nuclear-powered submarines. Rickover needed help to design, construct, test, and run them. He interviewed several officers, including Carter.

Inside the *K-1*, Carter studies some of the submarine's instruments.

Rickover grilled Carter for more than two hours. "He soon proved that I knew relatively little," Carter wrote in his memoir *Why Not the Best?* "I was saturated with cold sweat." When Rickover asked how he had done at the USNA, Carter proudly answered that he was ranked sixtieth in his class. He expected Rickover to congratulate him. Instead, Rickover asked, "Did you do your best?" Carter confessed, "No, sir, I didn't always do my best." "He looked at me for a long time, and then turned his chair around to end the interview. He asked one final question, which I have never been able to forget or to answer. He said, 'Why not?' I sat there for a while, shaken, and then slowly left the room."

Nonetheless, he got the job. On October 16, 1952, he joined Rickover's team at the United States Atomic Energy Commission's

Admiral Hyman Rickover was one of the most important people in Carter's life.

Division of Reactor Development and Technology in Schenectady, New York, more than 130 miles (210 km) northwest of New London. Rosalynn, Jack, and Chip joined him, along with someone new. On August 18, Rosalynn's twenty-fifth birthday, she had given birth to Donnel Jeffrey Carter, whom they called Jeff.

Carter didn't have much time for his sons. "[Rickover] demanded from me a standard of performance and a depth of commitment that I had never realized before that I could achieve," Carter said in the 1970s. "If I made the slightest mistake, in one of the loudest and most obnoxious voices I ever heard, he would turn around and tell the other people in the area what a horrible disgrace I was."

Carter hated Rickover's harshness, but he also admired the man. Rickover's nuclear vessels looked like the navy's future, and developing them could lead to Carter commanding his own submarine.

A GREAT LOSS AND A HOMECOMING

In the first half of 1953, Carter received a call from Plains. His father was dying of pancreatic cancer. The pancreas is a gland in the abdomen that issues fluids for the body to use in digestion. When cancer hits the pancreas, most people don't realize that they've got the disease until it spreads to other organs. By then, almost nothing can stop it from killing them.

When Carter heard the news, he lay across his bed and cried, then headed for Plains. Jimmy and Earl had never talked much. Whenever Carter had visited his father, the conversations usually ran along the lines of "You still like the navy?" "Yes, Daddy." Even as he lay dying, Earl didn't open his heart to his son.

Nonetheless, Carter learned a lot about Earl from the visit. People came from all over the area to thank Earl. His son heard them say that Earl had paid for their children's college tuition. He listened to poverty-burdened citizens who had borrowed money from Earl or rented homes

Once he learned of his father's illness, Carter returned home to Plains.

from him as they told how Earl had forgiven their debts or refused to take their rent payments. He listened to stories of Earl helping farmers and small businessmen suffering hard times. Earl had done it all secretly, without praise or publicity.

Carter compared his own life to Earl's. He was developing machines to kill his country's enemies, and he might eventually achieve fame and power, but Earl was quietly helping people feed their children and realize their dreams. The whole county seemed to be mourning Earl. When Jimmy died, would anyone care except his immediate family?

Earl died on July 22, 1953. Around that time, his oldest son decided to quit the navy, return to Plains, and take Earl's place. The decision cost him almost everything he had.

THREE

Plains, Peanuts, and Power

For seven years, Rosalynn had let her husband tell her what to do, but not this time. She cried, argued, screamed, and rebelled with everything she had to make Carter change his mind. No longer a shy teenager, she had raised three children on Carter's tiny salary while he spent months at sea. She had moved from town to town and battled loneliness each time. She had also seen more of the world than virtually anyone in Plains, and she couldn't stand the thought of going back. She even talked about divorcing her husband.

She didn't do it, despite her bitter misery. Many people with conservative values, including people in military families and people from rural Georgia, considered divorce shameful and nearly unthinkable. Besides, Rosalynn had three small children, few job skills, and nowhere to go for help except back to Plains.

On October 9, 1953, the navy gave Carter an honorable discharge. Now jobless, he moved his family into a cramped apartment in a government housing project for poor people. He took over Earl's businesses, including a peanut farm, a storage service that warehoused other farmers' crops, and a store that sold farm supplies, such as seed, feed, and fertilizer. Unfortunately, the economy was in a slump during 1953 and early 1954, and a drought in 1954 nearly ruined farming in southwestern Georgia. What's more, Carter found that Earl's generosity to the poor had nearly drained the family bank account. With no money to hire full-time help, Carter did nearly everything himself, from studying business management to loading bags of manure.

Eventually, he asked Rosalynn to keep track of the finances. Deadly bored with small-town life, Rosalynn happily agreed. They found that working together brought them closer.

AN IMPORTANT DECISION

Plains and other communities still kept black and white schoolchildren separate. In Topeka, Kansas, the father of black third-grader Linda Brown didn't like the situation and sued the board of education. The case went to the Supreme Court, which announced on May 17, 1954, "Segregation of white and Negro children in the public schools of a State solely on the basis of race . . . denies to Negro children the equal protection of the laws." No longer could schools legally segregate African Americans and whites.

The *Brown* v. *Board of Education* ruling infuriated many conservative southerners. Many of them formed White Citizens' Councils (WCC),

The Supreme Court declared school segregation was illegal in their decision in the *Brown* v. *Board of Education* case.

groups that opposed the ruling and sought ways to get around it. In Plains, the WCC included virtually every businessperson, including Carter's customers, and they asked him to join. Joining was easy and cheap, costing only $5. Refusing, they warned, meant that his customers might stop buying from him. Though the threat worried him, Carter said that he'd flush the money down the toilet before he'd give it to the WCC.

Some of Carter's customers deserted him, but they eventually came back. In 1956, Carter was making enough money to move his family from the housing project into a rented house not far from Lebanon Cemetery, where his father lay buried. They eventually tired of paying rent and in 1961 built a house in Plains—the only house they ever owned.

ENTERING POLITICS

The late 1950s and early 1960s passed quietly for Carter. His business continued to grow, as did his sons, while Rosalynn kept the house and account books.

Like Earl, Jimmy became involved in local politics. As the father of school-age boys, he cared about the area's schools and in 1955 joined Sumter County's Board of Education. To his disappointment, he found other board members trying to evade the *Brown* decision and keep the area's schools segregated. Nevertheless, he stayed on the job until 1962 and joined other local agencies, such as the local hospital board.

No matter how many local offices he held, Carter couldn't change the racist politicians that ruled the state. In 1962, "the leading candidate for governor of Georgia . . . threatened to close down any public school system with a single black child in it," Carter said thirty-five years later.

Very few institutions could stop the governor. However, one institution that could was the state senate. "I decided to run [for senator] just to protect the public school systems."

Carter's first campaign posters showed the young Democrat with a wide smile that became his trademark. He nailed the posters to signposts and trees, met groups of citizens, and applied all of his ferocious energy and discipline to winning. A primary election held on October 16 would eliminate all candidates but the two with the most votes, who would square off in the general election on November 6. In the primary, Carter had to unseat state senator Homer Moore, who had the support of the powerful political boss Joe Hurst.

Carter lost and suspected that there had been cheating. With John Pope, a friend and rural businessman like himself, Carter had watched the voting in Georgetown, a village under Hurst's control. Fewer than 350 people had voted, but the ballot box contained more than 400 votes. Someone had stuffed it with fakes.

Carter found an expert ally, lawyer Charles Kirbo, who had a quick mind and

This is one of Carter's campaign posters from the 1962 state senate election.

superb knowledge of Georgia's electoral laws. With Kirbo's help, Carter's team wrote a petition demanding that the government ignore Georgetown's votes. On October 20, they submitted the petition to Ben Fortson, Georgia's official in charge of elections. A day before the deadline for printing the general election ballots, Fortson certified Carter's claim.

Carter was put on the ballot. In the general election on November 6, Carter easily defeated Republican candidate Hal Suit. On January 14, 1963, Carter and other senators took the oath of office.

"He was not assertive," fellow senator Leroy Johnson said of Carter. "He was quiet, he was effective, he was deliberate, and he made no waves." In only a few areas did Carter stand out. He voted to remove laws that blocked black Georgians from voting. He supported President Lyndon B. Johnson, who favored equal rights for African-Americans.

The Vietnam War

The most troublesome issue of the 1960s was the Vietnam War. While the United States had had military advisors in South Vietnam for a number of years, the country did not become actively involved in the fighting until 1964. After North Vietnamese torpedo boats supposedly attacked U.S. destroyers in South Vietnam's Gulf of Tonkin, President Lyndon B. Johnson ordered air strikes against the North Vietnamese. Congress approved the Gulf of Tonkin Resolution, which allowed the president to take all actions necessary to win the war in Vietnam. By the end of 1965, more than 150,000 U.S. soldiers were serving there.

Joining the Corps

Lillian Carter had never stopped helping the helpless. In 1966, she saw a television commercial for the Peace Corps that changed her life. Peace Corps volunteers go to desperately poor places and do anything from nursing the sick to teaching English to helping farmers raise crops. Lillian, age sixty-seven, joined. The corps sent her to India. At first, she helped young Indians with family planning. Later, she switched to helping people with a disease called leprosy, which can cause physical disfigurement. She returned to Plains in 1968. When her son ran for president, nothing about her impressed people more than her service in the Peace Corps.

By 1966, Carter felt ready for new challenges. On June 12, he declared himself a candidate for governor.

Carter's most formidable opponents for the governorship were relatively moderate former governor Ellis Arnall and restaurant owner Lester Maddox, a racist. Maddox brandished an ax handle while campaigning and threatened to pound it into any African Americans who dared enter his restaurant. Carter, by contrast, courted the votes of liberals and African Americans.

In the primary election, both Arnall and Maddox won more votes than Carter did. In the general election, Maddox became governor. "The first real defeat of my life," Carter called the election in 1991. Until 1966, he had succeeded at every job he'd ever had. After years of rising in politics, he now felt condemned to selling peanuts until he died.

Losing the race for governor in 1966 was Carter's first big professional disappointment. This photograph shows Rosalynn and Jimmy Carter during the campaign.

DEPRESSION AND GROWTH

Carter's pain nearly destroyed his religious faith. As he said in 2001, "I felt I had been betrayed by God, that He had let a racist beat me."

Carter's sister Ruth had gone through her own time of spiritual emptiness. She had survived it by turning to God, and so she went to minister to her brother. During a walk in the woods near Plains, she quoted the Bible's Book of James: "My brethren, count it all joy when you fall into various trials." Ruth explained that surviving a painful time could give her brother patience and wisdom.

Carter turned to studying the Bible and devoting his life to Christ. He kept his businesses, but he also took on Christian missions. He traveled as far as Pennsylvania and Massachusetts to encourage others to take Christ into their lives.

He found a fresh start at home, too. In early 1967, Rosalynn announced that she was pregnant. On October 19, 1967, the Carters fulfilled a longstanding dream when Rosalynn gave birth to a daughter,

Amy Carter would grow up during much of her father's political career.

Amy Lynn. The baby, at least fifteen years younger than any of her brothers, would become the most famous Carter offspring.

Gradually, Carter returned to public affairs. He was still on the hospital board that he'd joined in the 1950s. He became president of the Georgia Planning Association, a group involved in land use and community development; and he became district governor of the Lions Clubs, a volunteer organization specializing in helping the blind. By 1968, he was even considering a new run for governor. The election would not take place until 1970, but he was already building a team to help him campaign.

Hamilton Jordan was a twenty-one-year-old University of Georgia student when he heard Carter give a speech during his first gubernatorial run. Politically active since childhood, always running for student offices or managing the campaigns of others, Jordan joined Carter's corps of volunteers and became one of its youngest leaders. When Carter prepared for another run, Jordan joined him and eventually became his campaign manager.

Joseph Powell, nicknamed Jody, was also a college student when he discovered Carter. In the late 1960s, Powell was studying political science at Atlanta's Emory University, where he researched Carter's 1966 campaign. Powell admired Carter and contacted him. By the end of 1968, at age twenty-five, Powell became Carter's personal assistant. He drove Carter to appointments, oversaw his schedule, and even brought him his meals.

Banker Bert Lance had met Carter in 1966 at a meeting of Georgia civic and financial leaders. Seven years younger than Carter, Lance had risen in the world of banking as Carter had succeeded in politics, by applying himself and working hard. The two became friends. When Carter decided to run for governor again, Lance offered his support.

SECOND TRY FOR GOVERNOR

On April 3, 1970, Carter announced his
candidacy to succeed Governor Maddox.
The governor wouldn't run against him; by
Georgia law, governors couldn't serve two
terms in a row. Carter's chief opponent for
the Democratic nomination was lawyer
Carl Sanders, Georgia's governor from 1963
through 1967. To beat Sanders, Carter pur-
sued white, working-class southerners.

To grab the votes of the white rural
voters and other poor and working-class
Georgians, Carter declared that Sanders was
too rich to care about the common voter.
To attract white voters in particular, Carter
courted the friendship of both Maddox and
the popular racist governor of neighboring
Alabama, George Wallace. He even refused
to criticize segregation openly.

In the primary on September 9, Carter
got more than 48 percent of the vote,
Sanders got less than 38 percent, and other
candidates split the rest. In the general election on November 3, Carter got 60 percent
of the vote against the Republican whom
he'd beaten in 1963, Hal Suit.

Once defeated, Carter
won the race for
governor in 1970.

Defeated in 1966, Carter emerged victorious this time. He had become Georgia's governor.

GOVERNOR JIMMY

At his inauguration on January 12, 1971, Carter declared, "The time for racial discrimination is over." Coming from a Georgia governor, the words provoked nationwide surprise. *The New York Times,* one of the nation's most respected newspapers, put Carter's inaugural address on page one. On May 31, the powerful and popular *Time* magazine put Carter's face on the cover and named him a leader among a new wave of progressive southern governors.

Carter put some of his closest advisors into office. Though Jody Powell was only twenty-seven, which is very young to wield power in government, he became Carter's press secretary. He was in charge of presenting Carter's policies and activities to journalists and the public. Hamilton Jordan, a year younger than Powell, became Carter's executive secretary. In this position, Jordan would be the person whom legislators

Younger Voters

In 1971, an amendment was made to the Constitution to lower the legal voting age from twenty-one to eighteen. This amendment provided young people with the opportunity to become more active in the political process, and many of them would vote for Carter.

and others had to contact in order to reach the governor. Bert Lance became director of highways and transportation, but his most important job was as Carter's most respected advisor and closest friend.

Carter loved being governor. "That was one of the most pleasant four years of my life," he said in 1982. By most measures, he did the job well. "When I took over, we had a bureaucratic mess," he said while running for president in 1976. Multiple government divisions oversaw the same areas, which led to bickering and waste. Within a month of taking office, Carter pushed the first of several bills through the legislature to eliminate some agencies and combine others.

Carter sought to improve the criminal justice system as well, especially the prisons. Prison officials punished convicts far more brutally than their sentences allowed, and Carter worked to clean up the system. When he found that many prisoners committed crimes after their release, he set up education programs to help them get honest jobs after prison.

Most of the prisoners who received the worst treatment were African American. At the same time, Georgia's state government hired few if any black employees. Outraged, Carter put African Americans on important boards and commissions, and raised the number of black government employees from less than five thousand to more than six thousand.

Carter also reformed the state's welfare system, which should have given aid to the poor but had become a swamp of endless paperwork. He tightened environmental controls to reduce pollution. He invited foreign countries to build factories in Georgia, which not only attracted money and jobs but also taught him how to work with leaders outside of his own region. He saved money wherever he could. He even made legislators and others who came for lunch meetings pay for their own food rather than let the state cover the costs.

He made enemies, but not just because people disagreed with his policies. When a typical politician wants legislators to pass a law, he or she might remove parts of the law they dislike or offer a deal they do like, such as promising to vote in support of another bill. Not Carter. His staff came to dread the icy glare in his blue eyes when anyone suggested a compromise or trade-off.

"If you happened to agree with him, he thought you were one of God's chosen tribe—but if you didn't, you were automatically in league with the devil," one of his opponents told journalist James Wooten. "I'd never be able to disagree with him without him taking out after me like an avenging angel."

As governor, Carter sought to make changes to improve how the state government operated, cut costs, and protected the environment.

PRESIDENT JIMMY?

The early 1970s saw Carter enter into national affairs. A presidential election would take place in 1972, and candidates came to court his support. By the end of 1971, Carter had met President Richard Nixon, several prominent senators, and a number of other state governors. "I began comparing my own experience and knowledge of government with the candidates'," he said years later. He realized that he could match them in most areas and outdo them in hard work and self-discipline.

Carter felt that the leading contender for 1972's Democratic presidential candidate, South Dakota senator George McGovern, was too liberal to unseat President Richard Nixon. Carter supported a movement to block McGovern from winning the nomination. His efforts failed, and Nixon trounced McGovern in a landslide victory.

Carter started thinking about life after 1975, when his term as governor would have ended. So did his staff and advisors. Early in autumn of 1972, Hamilton Jordan led a group of them to encourage Carter to run for president in the next election. They didn't realize that he had already decided to run.

Hamilton Jordan was an important member of the staff in Carter's presidential campaign.

FOUR

"My Name Is Jimmy Carter"

The presidency seemed unattainable. The American people hadn't elected a governor to be president since 1932. They hadn't elected a southerner to be president since 1848. What's more, in 1972, Carter had been running the state of Georgia for less than two years and had no experience with national politics at all. Most Americans had never even heard of him.

Carter assigned Jordan to write a plan that would push him into the White House. Jordan finished it in November 1973. About seventy pages long, the document changed American politics.

Among other things, Jordan's plan called for Carter to make himself prominent among America's most powerful people. Carter therefore joined the Trilateral Commission. "Trilateral" means "three-sided." Banker David Rockefeller started the commission in 1973 to foster cooperation among business executives and other leaders in three centers of democracy and big business: Japan, Western Europe, and the English-speaking countries of North America. For director of the organization, Rockefeller selected Columbia University professor Zbigniew Brzezinski. An expert on foreign policy, Brzezinski had advised President Johnson and Vice President Hubert Humphrey. He was looking for rising political stars to join the commission when he found Carter.

The Trilateral Commission helped Carter develop knowledge of foreign affairs and introduced him to powerful leaders. He grew especially close to Brzezinski. He admired the professor's intellect and hard-line opposition to the Soviet Union. Eventually, he asked Brzezinski to join his presidential campaign as the top foreign-policy advisor.

Carter also reached into the Democratic Party for campaign help. Political commentators sometimes called Robert Strauss "Mr. Democrat." The Texas lawyer had advised powerful Democratic politicians since the 1930s. During 1972, Carter and Strauss had worked together in the anti-McGovern movement. Later that year, Strauss became the party's chairman. He knew that in 1974, every seat in the House of Representatives and a third of the Senate would be up for reelection. He named Carter the national campaign chairman, assigning him to help Democrats raise money, hold rallies, and do anything else to get votes. The job perfectly suited Carter, who wanted Democrats to support his presidential ambitions.

One Democrat who supported Carter was Patrick Caddell, McGovern's chief pollster. A South Carolinian in his mid-twenties, Caddell seemed a worthy partner for Jordan and Powell. He helped them understand the moods and attitudes of the American people.

According to Caddell's findings, Americans wanted a new voice in the government. Throughout the past decade, racism and other problems had caused conflicts ranging from dinner-table arguments to college-campus riots. The harshest fights concerned the Vietnam War. In the late 1960s and early 1970s, thousands of Americans died in the first war that the United States had ever lost.

The Vietnam War soured Americans' faith in their leaders, but even more trouble was coming. In 1972 President Nixon authorized a burglary of the Democratic National Committee's offices in Washington, D.C.'s

The Watergate Scandal

In June 1972, five burglars broke into the Democratic National Committee headquarters and were caught by the police. They were tried along with two others on charges of burglary, conspiracy, and wiretapping. There was some evidence that the criminals had ties to the Committee to Re-elect the President. It was later discovered that President Nixon had been involved in the efforts to cover up the crime. In 1974, the House Judiciary Committee recommended that Nixon be impeached for abusing presidential powers, obstructing justice, and interfering in the impeachment process by defying committee subpoenas.

Watergate building complex. He and his accomplices covered up the crime and lied about the cover-up. The House of Representatives was on the verge of impeaching Nixon when he resigned on August 9, 1974.

Vice President Gerald Ford became president. The United States welcomed the unpretentious Ford until September 8. "The tranquility to which this nation has been restored by the events of recent weeks could be irreparably lost by the prospects of bringing to trial a former president," Ford declared on that day. "Therefore, I . . . grant a full, free, and absolute pardon unto Richard Nixon." Many Americans hated seeing Nixon escape punishment and were unhappy with Ford's actions.

For their next president, Americans wanted an honest man who would give them, in the words of his campaign slogan, "a government as good as its people." They didn't know it yet, but they wanted Carter.

On December 12, 1974, at the prestigious National Press Club in Washington, D.C., Carter declared publicly for the first time that he was running for president. Nobody cared. The journalists couldn't believe that a little-known peanut farmer could win the Democratic nomination in July of 1976, much less the general election in November.

To promote himself, Carter wrote an autobiography, which the Baptist Sunday School Board published in 1975. He called the book *Why Not the Best?*, after the question posed by Hyman Rickover that had shaken young Lieutenant Carter.

When his term as governor ended in mid-January of 1975, Carter hit the road. He met voters wherever he could, greeting them simply, "My name is Jimmy Carter, and I'm running for President." Depressingly often, the voters responded, "Jimmy who?"

The campaign didn't have much money. Carter saved on lodging and stayed in touch with ordinary Americans by sleeping in the homes of his supporters. Some of the supporters were enthusiastic Georgia volunteers whom called themselves the "peanut brigade."

Among Carter's most important supporters were African American civil rights crusaders Andrew Young and Martin Luther King, Sr. Carter had known Young since 1970, when they were both running for office. Young eventually became Georgia's first black congressman in nearly a century. Starting in 1975, he helped Carter's nearly all-white team reach people of color.

By the end of the year, though, polls showed Carter badly trailing better-known Democrats such as Hubert Humphrey. Fortunately for Carter, however, the world of politics was changing. Candidates used to get their party's nomination through the states' top politicians. Each local leader would select delegates to vote for his candidate at their party's national convention. In the wake of the Watergate scandal and an overall distrust

A lot of Carter's support came from volunteers who called themselves the peanut brigade.

of political insiders, more and more states let voters pick delegates directly. While candidates who worked the old way didn't even put their names on some states' ballots, Carter's team fought hard to get voter support everywhere.

The first state to vote, Iowa, held a caucus on January 19, 1976. "When voters cast their ballots in the Iowa caucus, they won't be doing it in the privacy of a booth," said the Public Broadcasting System's respected *NewsHour*. "Instead, they gather in places such as school gymnasiums and fire halls to join fellow supporters of a particular candidate. For the Democrats, the groups divide in the room, while encouraging undecideds to join them. Their numbers are then tallied."

Carter won. He took 27.6 percent of the vote, which put him well ahead of the other candidates. Though the largest group of voters, 37.2 percent, voted "undecided," the press dubbed Carter the winner.

NEW HAMPSHIRE

Suddenly, the nation's attention focused on Carter. Donors offered him money, and new supporters signed up to help his campaign. Carter needed them, especially in the upcoming primaries.

Primaries mattered more than caucuses. Only the most politically active citizens vote in caucuses, and their delegates can sometimes change their minds and switch candidates. Many more voters cast ballots in primaries, and their delegates usually stay committed.

The first primary took place in New Hampshire on February 24. Carter put in long days, plugging through snowstorms to speak to group after group of Democrats. Rarely had he benefited so much from the work habits that his father and the navy had taught him. Carter got 23,373 votes and took first place by more than 5 percentage points over the nearest other candidate. "Jimmy Who?" became the front-runner.

Carter emphasized his personality and moral beliefs more than his views on issues. He also advertised his family. Americans respected Rosalynn's quiet grace and the obvious warmth that she and her husband shared. They loved Amy's spunk and cuteness. They marveled at

During the campaign, Carter and his family received a lot of media attention. Here, Jimmy and Rosalynn pose for a photograph during one of his campaign trips.

Jimmy's sisters. Ruth was a devout minister, and Gloria was an avid motorcycle rider who still roared around the countryside in her fifties. They delighted at 78-year-old Lillian's tart talk. Lillian was famous for lines such as "Sure, I'm for helping the elderly. I'm going to be old myself someday." Finally, they couldn't get enough of his wisecracking brother Billy.

CONVENTIONAL WISDOM

Carter won primary after primary. After the last of the primaries ended on June 8, he prepared for the Democratic National Convention on July 12 through 15, when his party would formally nominate him. His most important task was choosing a running mate for vice president.

Ethnic Purity

Carter was riding high on April 2 when he told a reporter for the *New York Daily News* that he wouldn't force neighborhoods to include residents of different races. As he put it, he would allow black neighborhoods, Hispanic neighborhoods, and others to maintain "ethnic purity." The phrase sounded like a defense of segregation.

African Americans and others protested until Andrew Young spoke up. He helped Carter apologize, and the scandal passed. It was the first big, well-publicized mistake that Carter made during the campaign, and no one involved ever forgot it.

He chose Walter Mondale. The liberal senator from Minnesota didn't know Carter well, but when they discussed the job, "he was completely frank about assessing his own strengths and weaknesses," Carter wrote in one of his memoirs. "I felt he would be adequately independent and adequately loyal." Not exactly a vow of brotherhood, but it was enough.

On July 15, Carter entered New York City's Madison Square Garden. With thousands in the arena and millions watching on television, he ascended the podium and gave a speech to accept his party's nomination. He began with the words that he'd said so often: "My name is Jimmy Carter, and I'm running for president."

"It's been a long time since I said those words the first time," he went on. "It is time for America to move and to speak, not with boasting and belligerence but with a quiet strength, to depend in world affairs not merely on the size of an arsenal but on the nobility of ideas, and to govern at home not by confusion and

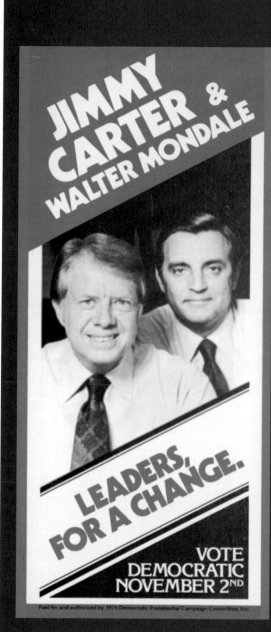

Jimmy Carter chose Walter Mondale to be his running mate.

crisis but with grace and imagination and common sense." When pollsters asked voters if they preferred Carter or his Republican opponent, President Ford, more Americans picked Carter. Carter had a lead of about 20 to 30 percent, depending on the poll.

RISING TO POWER

In August came the Republicans' convention. On its last night, Ford performed as impressively as Carter had at the Democratic affair, and Americans started to think Republican. Carter had to stop them.

His first big chance came on September 23, when he met Ford for the first of three televised debates. "There was an aura about the presidency that was quite overwhelming," Carter confessed in 1989. "[I had] an insecure feeling about being placed, at least for that hour and a half, on an equal basis with the president."

The first debate covered domestic issues such as taxes, jobs, housing, and energy. Overshadowing the candidates' statements, though, was an audio-equipment failure that cut off the debate for twenty-seven minutes while Carter and Ford simply stood at their podiums. Neither of them looked very presidential.

During the second debate on October 6, Carter made a better showing. He and Ford discussed foreign affairs. Though Eastern Europe lay under the Soviet Union's control, Ford declared, "There is no Soviet domination of Eastern Europe." Many Americans already considered Ford less than bright, and his statement supported their suspicions.

As the November 2 election day approached, opinion polls showed Ford and Carter to be nearly tied. On the day itself, Carter voted in

Atlanta and waited for the results. The final tally gave Ford 39,145,977 votes and Carter 40,827,394—one of the tightest presidential races in American history.

Late that night, Carter and Rosalynn took a train to Plains. When they arrived the next morning, virtually everyone from the area was waiting for them. Carter knew nearly every face, and the experience of coming home after his greatest triumph overcame him. The boy who pushed himself endlessly to gain his father's love, the teenager who endured the rigors of the USNA, the man who labored to rebuild his father's dying business, and the small-time politician who ran for govenor had just attained the nation's most important post. Jimmy Carter looked out on the hometown that he'd left years before and cried.

During the campaign, Carter faced off with President Ford in a series of televised debates.

Jimmy Carter took the oath of office on January 20, 1977, becoming the thirty-ninth president of the United States.

FIVE

President Jimmy

Supreme Court Chief Justice Warren Burger would swear Carter into office on January 20, 1977. Carter had less than three months to prepare for the nation's most important job. His first priority was to hire a staff.

To run the Office of Management and Budget, which oversaw a wide swath of government spending and organization, he picked Bert Lance. He chose Jody Powell to be his press secretary. Hamilton Jordan eventually became the chief of staff.

Another trusted advisor already had a job. Many presidents ignored their vice presidents, assigning them empty jobs, such as attending foreign statesmen's funerals. Instead, as Mondale said in 2000, "I was the first vice president to have an office in the White House, to be privy to the full scope of the work of the president." Carter consulted the experienced Washington insider often, and their relationship became the new standard for presidents and vice presidents.

To suggest candidates for jobs in foreign affairs, Carter turned to Zbigniew Brzezinski. For secretary of state, Brzezinski helped him select Cyrus Vance, a lawyer who had served in the Defense Department, had negotiated peace treaties, and had advised Carter during the campaign. For representative to the United Nations, Carter picked Andrew Young. As for Brzezinski himself, Carter named him national security advisor, a leading counselor on military and foreign affairs.

Carter's most important advisor, he soon realized, lived with him. "The first year Jimmy was in office, I became so frustrated," Rosalynn said years later. "Every night, Jimmy would get off the elevator at the White House, and I would say, 'Why did you do this?' or 'Why did you do something?' And one day, he finally said, 'Why don't you come to Cabinet meetings? Then you'll know why we do these things.'" The first presidential wife to attend the meetings regularly, Rosalynn soon took on issues of her own, speaking out strongly for the elderly and the mentally ill.

After the election, Carter often met with people in town meetings to hear their concerns.

HUMBLE BEGINNINGS

On Inauguration Day, standing in the cold midday air before the Capitol building, Carter recited the presidential oath: "I do solemnly swear that I will faithfully execute the office of the President of the United States, and will, to the best of my ability, preserve, protect, and defend the Constitution of the United States." He faced a crowd of dignitaries, political supporters, and thousands of others and began his inaugural address.

"For myself and for our nation, I want to thank my predecessor for all he has done to heal our land [after Watergate and Vietnam]. . . .

"I join in the hope that when my time as your President has ended, people might say . . . that we had enabled our people to be proud of their own government once again."

After the speech, the Carters did what other First Families had done on Inauguration Day. They got into a limousine heading for the White House. Before it went far, though, they got out and walked. Their stroll down Pennsylvania Avenue showed Carter as a man of the people, walking among them in the open air rather than riding isolated in luxury. The walk became one of the decade's most famous images.

After the inauguration, Carter enjoyed a long period of popularity. To keep in close touch with the people, during March he held a nationwide broadcast in which Americans phoned in questions for him to answer. Later that month, he appeared at a "town meeting" in Clinton, Massachusetts, to talk with Americans face-to-face. By the middle of 1977, 70 percent or more of the American people approved of him.

Then he hit trouble. Carter had campaigned against many Washington insiders. When he became president, his team tried to govern the same way and didn't build effective alliances with members of Congress. Carter didn't help matters with his refusal to compromise for political gain, his impatience with Congress' slow pace, and his disgust with politicians who approved costly, wasteful projects simply because the projects poured money into their home districts. In turn, many members of Congress considered Carter self-righteous and inflexible.

Unfortunately, Carter needed Congress's help. "We tried to do too much too fast," he admitted in 1982. The White House sent Congress proposals to control health-care costs, reorganize the government, reform the system of welfare payments to poor Americans, eliminate some dams and other water projects, and create a new, cabinet-level Department of Energy to handle matters of fuel and power.

Fuel and power were especially important because the winter of 1976–1977 saw shortages of natural gas fuel that kept Americans warm. On February 2, after he signed the Emergency National Gas Act "to order emergency deliveries and transportation of natural gas," Carter made his first speech since the inauguration. Sitting near a cozy fireplace rather than behind a desk and wearing an informal sweater instead of a suit, Carter asked Americans to conserve power. "Simply by keeping our thermostats, for instance, at sixty-five degrees in the daytime and fifty-five degrees at night, we can save half the current shortage of natural gas."

Americans liked Carter's humble style but didn't support his energy policies. Though he presented a comprehensive energy bill to Congress in March and on April 18 described the effort to improve the energy situation as "the moral equivalent of war," the bill stalled in Congress for months. So did many of his other proposals.

GETTING LANCED

Carter's best friend caused him even more headaches. Before joining the Carter Administration, Bert Lance had been chairman of the National Bank of Georgia. He bought stock in the bank for $3.3 million. Later, when he became a government official, he wasn't allowed to own that stock anymore. Lance had to sell his shares by the end of 1977.

By July, though, the bank's worth had fallen, cutting the value of Lance's shares nearly in half. If he sold his stock by the deadline, he would lose $1.6 million. Carter asked Congress to give Lance more time, but the request seemed like a powerful man trying to bend the rules for a friend. What's more, government investigators found that Lance borrowed money from his own bank, the Calhoun National Bank. The bank had lent him the money with better terms than it gave other borrowers. Better terms could have included getting better interest rates or not being charged certain fees.

The federal Comptroller of the Currency supervises the banking system. On August 18, the comptroller cleared Lance of any crime. Carter publicly declared, "Bert, I am proud of you." Unfortunately, the comptroller also accused Lance of "unsafe and unsound banking practices." Journalists, government officials, and many Americans accused both Lance and Carter of corruption. On September 21, Lance resigned. The scandal affected the public's trust in Carter and made him more cautious and defensive in domestic affairs.

TACKLING FOREIGN AFFAIRS

Carter turned to foreign affairs. His strong moral code made him want to guarantee human rights to other nations. Unfortunately, the United States had supported leaders who violated human rights, if they joined the United States in opposing communism and the Soviet Union. On May 22, Carter's first presidential foreign-policy speech tackled the situation. "We are now free of that inordinate fear of communism which once led us to embrace any dictator who joined us."

The speech drew the criticism that Carter didn't oppose the Soviet Union and other communist nations strongly enough. He angered his critics even more in June when he blocked the construction of powerful bombers called B-1s. As time passed, many Americans would believe that Carter was too soft to counter the Soviet drive to spread communism worldwide.

TREATIES WITH PANAMA

For centuries, ships leaving North America's Atlantic Coast had to sail around South America to reach Pacific ports. In 1914, the U.S. government completed a canal through the Latin American nation of Panama. The waterway reduced the trip from nearly 8,000 miles (12,874 km) to about 40 miles (64 km).

The U.S. government controlled the Panama Canal and the land around it. The situation infuriated the people of Panama, who felt that they should control any canal located on their land. Other Latin American nations agreed.

For decades, the United States had been negotiating treaties to give control of the canal to the Panamanians. On September 7, 1977, Carter signed the treaties with Panama's ruler, Omar Torrijos. Treaties require Senate approval, though, and many senators and other Americans disliked the treaty. They agreed with conservative California governor Ronald Reagan when he said in 1976, "We built it, we paid for it, it's ours, and we're going to keep it."

Only after Carter fought and defeated the anti-treaty forces did the Senate finally approve the treaties, accepting the last of them on April 18, 1978. The battle used up a lot of Carter's "political capital," a combination of popularity and force that encourages people to follow a leader. It also helped make Carter look like he was caving in to foreign pressure.

A NATION IN HARD TIMES

During much of the time Carter was in office, the United States was experiencing economic trouble. Through a process called inflation, prices rose

The Panama Canal

The United States began work on the Pamana Canal in 1904. To create it, workers had dig the canal through difficult terrain, such as swamps and mountains infested with disease-carrying insects. The project was finished in 1914. The canal provided a shortcut for ships to get between the Atlantic and Pacific Oceans.

faster than most Americans could handle. The number of jobless Americans was rising, too.

Carter's advisors seemed unable to improve the situation. Many influential Washingtonians considered his senior aides too inexperienced and undisciplined to run the government. By the summer of 1978, most Americans were saying that they disliked the president. As it happened, it was time for his greatest triumph.

CAMP DAVID

Jews, Muslims, and Christians have battled for centuries to control the land that is currently Israel. The land has religious significance to all three groups. Some of the groups don't accept that any other has a right to rule the land or live there at all. Things became especially explosive after 1967's Six-Day War, when Israel conquered large swaths of land

Getting the leaders of Egypt and Israel to discuss peace was a huge accomplishment for Carter. This photograph shows Anwar Sadat, Jimmy Carter, and Menachem Begin holding a meeting outside at Camp David.

formerly controlled by neighboring Arab nations, such as Egypt. The nearby Arab nations wanted to destroy Israel. Israel wanted to rule the conquered lands occupied by Arabs called Palestinians. President after president tried to negotiate peace among the Israeli government and the Arab nations. Secretary of State Vance wrote in his memoirs, "Failure [to negotiate a peace] could lead to the overthrow of moderate Arab leaders, the strengthening of anti-Western Arab radicals, an increase in Soviet influence, [and] a return to the brink of war."

In November 1977, Egyptian president Anwar Sadat visited Israeli prime minister Menachem Begin in Jerusalem, and became the first Arab leader to enter Israel. Begin responded by visiting Egypt's capital, Cairo. Afterwards, though, peace negotiations stalled until August 1978, when Carter invited Begin and Sadat to talk at Camp David.

The cool, tranquil forest resort lies in Maryland's Catoctin Mountains, about 70 miles (115 km) northwest of Washington, D.C. Since the 1940s, presidents have visited its quiet paths and cozy cabins to negotiate with foreign leaders, plot political strategy, or simply stroll, bicycle, fish, or picnic. Carter thought Camp David's calm, informal atmosphere made it a perfect place to talk about peace.

The talks started on September 5 and nearly ended several times during the next few days. Carter felt that Sadat was too ready to return to Egypt when talks broke down, but he considered Sadat a true peacemaker who could compromise enough to reach an agreement. By contrast, Carter saw Begin as a hard-line extremist who argued endlessly over every word. At least once, Carter shouted at Begin. More than once, Begin shouted at Carter and Sadat.

On September 17, to the world's surprise, the three leaders announced that an agreement. Under Carter's leadership, a team of American

Chinese leader Deng Xiaoping and his wife visited the Carters at the White House in 1979.

negotiators had written a peace proposal. After revisions by Begin and Sadat, it became "A Framework for Peace in the Middle East," also called the Camp David Accords. Under the accords, Egypt became the first Arab nation to recognize officially that Israel's government was the legitimate ruler of its land. Egypt was also the first to make peace with Israel rather than just a temporary cease-fire. In exchange, Israel agreed to give back much of the land that it had taken from Egypt. The accords skirted a number of touchy points on which neither Sadat nor Begin would budge, such as who would control the holy city of Jerusalem, but both sides remained willing to discuss those issues.

Ever since, nearly everyone who has tried to negotiate Israeli–Arab relations has used the Camp David Accords as a starting point.

SUCCESS IN INTERNATIONAL RELATIONS

After Camp David, many Americans saw Carter as a hero. On October 15, 1978, Congress even passed a version of the comprehensive energy bill that he had proposed in the spring of 1977.

Two months later, Carter took a foreign-policy step almost as bold as the Camp David Accords.

In 1949, communist Chinese revolutionaries had overthrown their nation's government. The previous leaders, whom the U.S. government counted as allies, fled to the nearby island of Taiwan. The United States considered the Taiwan group China's only legitimate government and wouldn't accept the communists as rulers.

Starting in 1972, presidents Nixon and Ford had reached out to the communists. Carter carried on their work. On December 15, 1978, he announced that the United States would formally recognize the communists as China's true leaders. In his autobiography, Secretary of State Vance called the announcement "one of the enduring achievements of the Carter years."

Carter was able to reach an agreement with Leonid Brezhnev on limiting the number of weapons that the United States and the Soviet Union had.

Gas stations often ran out of gas during the shortage of 1979.

Soon afterwards, Carter scored another triumph. In the early 1970s, President Nixon and Soviet leader Leonid Brezhncv had started the Strategic Arms Limitation Talks (SALT). In May of 1972, they signed a treaty to limit the growth of their nuclear arsenals. The treaty would eventually expire, though, and Brzezinski, Vance, and other members of Carter's foreign-policy team had been trying since early 1977 to negotiate a new one. Finally, on June 18, 1979, Carter and Brezhnev signed SALT II. The treaty intended "to limit strategic offensive arms quantitatively and qualitatively, [and] to exercise restraint in the development of new types of strategic offensive arms."

To millions, Carter's overtures to Russia, China, and other countries polished his reputation as a peacemaker. Others, though, saw him as a naïve weakling who traded America's safety for some empty promises.

MALAISE AND RESIGNATIONS

By mid-1979, a number of pressing issues were affecting Americans. Inflation remained high, and the number of people out of work kept increasing. Shortages of oil were shooting petroleum prices skyward, pushing up the price of everything from fuel for home heating to food and other products delivered by truck. People also had to wait in long lines at gas stations to fuel their cars. Americans became disenchanted with Carter. As Patrick Caddell said, "The country is having this terrible domestic problem, and the President is somewhere out on the other side of the world."

On July 3, 1979, Carter went to Camp David for meetings on America's problems, known as a "domestic summit." He spent days listening to more than a hundred politicians, clergymen, union leaders, corporate heads, and others tell him what he was doing wrong. On July 15, he went on national television to reveal what he had learned.

"The true problems of our nation are much deeper than gasoline lines or energy shortages," he said. "The threat is nearly invisible in ordinary ways. It is a crisis of confidence. It is a crisis that strikes at the very heart and soul and spirit of our national will. We can see this crisis in the growing doubt about the meaning of our own lives and in the loss of a unity of purpose for our nation." Carter viewed the speech as a call to action: "I need your help. . . . Whenever you have a chance, say something good about our country."

Some Americans came to view the speech as Carter's confession that he couldn't handle the nation's problems. The talk became known as the "malaise" (meaning exhaustion and discomfort) speech, even though Carter didn't use that word. It reinforced his reputation as weak and inept.

The speech contained a comment made at the domestic summit: "Some of your Cabinet members don't seem loyal." Carter asked his cabinet and senior staff to resign, an act that struck much of the public as heavy-handed and unnecessary. By late July, Carter decided to keep most of his people in their jobs, but he dropped his treasury secretary, attorney general, transportation secretary, and health, education, and welfare secretary, among others.

United Nations Ambassador Andrew Young soon joined them. Young often spoke publicly on American policy without consulting the president and even criticized his own country for human-rights violations. The last straw involved the Palestine Liberation Organization, a group of terrorists and others who sought nationhood for Palestinians and accused Israel of violating Palestinian rights. The U.S. government had forbidden its officials to meet PLO representatives. In July 1979, Young met with PLO members and even seemed to sympathize with them. The meeting produced so much fury among American supporters of Israel that on August 15, Young resigned.

Even worse news was coming, though.

SHAH AND AYATOLLAH

Though Carter usually denounced dictators, he befriended Iran's shah (king), Reza Shah Pahlavi. Iran meant a lot to the United States. It bordered both the Middle East and the Soviet Union and stood as one of the United States's few friends in the region. At the same time, Pahlavi's national organization for intelligence and security, called Sazeman-i Ettelaat va Amniyat-i Keshvar (SAVAK), imprisoned, tortured, and killed Iranians who disagreed with him.

Nevertheless, anti-shah protests increased throughout 1978. Some of the loudest protestors were fanatically devout Muslim priests. When the shah aimed SAVAK at them, Iran's mostly Muslim populace rioted.

On January 16, 1979, the shah fled the country. The radical Muslims replaced him with Ruhollah Khomeini, a grim, aged ayatollah (religious leader).

By the summer of 1979, the shah was dying. He had lymphatic cancer, which strikes bodily systems that repel sickness. New York Hospital provided some of the world's best cancer treatments, but a widely hated ex-king couldn't enter a U.S. city without government permission. Friends of the shah, including Trilateral Commission founder David Rockefeller, pushed Carter to admit him. On October 22, Carter did so.

Iranians hit the streets in protest. On November 4, a group of at least three thousand rioting college students invaded the U.S. embassy compound in Tehran, Iran's capital. Inside the embassy were more than sixty Americans, plus other non-Iranians. The students took them all hostage.

The Iranian hostage crisis would be one of the greatest challenges of Carter's presidency.

Outside, angry Iranians burned American flags and yelled that America was "the Great Satan."

No mob had ever overrun a U.S. embassy before. Carter considered sending soldiers to retake the embassy, but he realized that the students might kill the hostages if soldiers came near. Instead, he froze the assets that Iran's government had deposited in U.S. banks, cutting the country off from much of its wealth. On November 17, the students freed thirteen African American and female hostages. From then on, though, they refused to budge.

THE CRISIS CONTINUES

Carter's representatives negotiated with Iranian leaders throughout late 1979 and early 1980, but nothing worked. Finally, Carter sent in the military. On April 24, 1980, eight American helicopters and six planes secretly landed in

Afghanistan Invaded

In December, a crisis hit one of Iran's neighbors. Afghanistan was a crucial gateway between much of the Middle East and Asia. On its northern border lay the Soviet Union. Afghanistan's government allied itself with the Soviets, but many of its citizens were Muslim fundamentalists. Like the Iranians under the shah, the Afghan Muslims staged uprisings against their ruler. By late 1979, they were waging all-out war to take over the government. Soviet leader Leonid Brezhnev didn't want another Islamic regime on his border. On Christmas Day, 1979, the Soviet army invaded Afghanistan.

the Iranian desert. The plan was to load the helicopters with soldiers and fly them into the embassy compound. The soldiers would rescue the hostages and take them to the desert, where the planes would fly them home.

Before the helicopters could take off, though, a sandstorm hit, and two helicopters malfunctioned. Carter cancelled the mission. Minutes later, his phone rang. "He paled visibly," reported Secretary of State Vance. "A helicopter had collided with one of our [planes] loaded with men." Eight soldiers died. "That was perhaps the high point of despair in my presidency," Carter said in 2002.

RUNNING FOR REELECTION

Amid his other chores in 1980, Carter was running for reelection. By the Democratic National Convention in August, most public-opinion polls tied Carter with his Republican opponent, Ronald Reagan, or gave the president a slight advantage.

Reagan, a former actor who starred in many Westerns, presented himself as friendly, strong, and optimistic. As the United States suffered high unemployment and high prices, Reagan asked his audiences, "Are you

The Iran-Iraq War

Though the United States didn't attack Iran, another country did. On Iran's southwestern border lay Iraq. Iraq's ruler, the power-hungry Saddam Hussein, had long wanted to conquer Iran. At the same time, Khomeini had encouraged Iraq's fundamentalist Muslims to overthrow Hussein by supporting anti-Hussein uprisings among Iraq's Kurds, a rebellious ethnic minority. On September 22, 1980, Iraq invaded Iran. The attack strained Iran in ways that would change Carter's presidency.

better off now than you were four years ago?" He promised to fix their financial problems by cutting taxes and reducing the size of the government. As Carter struggled with Iran and the Soviets, Reagan pledged to build up America's armed forces and make other nations respect the United States. While Carter's "malaise" speech warned of "the erosion of our confidence in the future," Reagan argued, "The confidence we have lost is confidence in our government's policies" and promised, "We will become [a] shining city on a hill."

Carter's campaign speeches portrayed Reagan as a dangerously unrealistic ultra-conservative who preferred wielding force to negotiating treaties and defending human rights. He also felt that Reagan's tax cuts would eliminate government programs that protected the health and safety of the people.

On October 28, a week before the election, Carter met Reagan for their only televised debate. Reagan seemed warm, forthright, and mature, not wild or radical. When Carter criticized Reagan for opposing national health care, Reagan chided him, "There you go again, Mr. President." To some people, the line made Carter look like a reckless attacker repeating a series of false accusations.

Carter and Reagan debated on television only a week before the election.

Later in the debate, Carter said, "I had a discussion with my daughter, Amy, the other day before I came here to ask her what the most important issue was. She said she thought nuclear weaponry and the control of nuclear arms." Carter may have been trying to appear friendly and fatherly, but the idea of a president consulting a teenager on world affairs struck some voters as ridiculous.

THE END OF A PRESIDENCY

If the debate didn't seal the election, a grisly coincidence did. Election Day, November 4, marked exactly one year since the Iranian students had taken the Americans hostage. The press always emphasizes anniversaries. "A good portion of that weekend leading up to it," Jody Powell later said, "Americans were literally having their nose rubbed in this embarrassing, irritating, humiliating situation."

By Election Day, Carter was a heap of exhaustion and resentment. He felt even worse that night, when he took only 41 percent and Reagan took 51 percent of the vote. He was still president until January 20, though. He sent Congress environmental bills to protect huge tracts of Alaska and to set aside a "superfund" of money for cleaning up some polluted areas. Before he left office, Congress passed them into law.

Mostly, Carter worked on freeing the hostages. "In the last three days I was president, I didn't go to bed at all," he said in 2002. "I stayed up to negotiate in the most frustrating way."

On January 19, Carter announced that he had succeeded. So had Khomeini. With a war in Iraq demanding his attention and a new and unfamiliar president taking power, Khomeini decided that the hostages had become more trouble than they were worth. Still, he stretched the negotiations almost to the moment when Reagan took his oath of office, thereby humiliating Carter. Only after Chief Justice Burger swore Reagan in as president did the ayatollah let the hostages in Iran go.

The Iranians flew the hostages to an U.S. Air Force base in Wiesbaden, Germany. President Reagan sent Carter to welcome them. It was Carter's first public act as a newly private citizen.

SIX

Plains and the World

When Jimmy, Rosalynn, and Amy Carter arrived in Plains, they looked out over a field of umbrellas. Thousands of people were standing in the rain to welcome them home.

On his first full day back in the house he'd bought in 1961, the former president went to a lumberyard and bought strips of wood. Carter enjoyed woodworking and planned to build a new floor in the attic. Eventually, he would craft pieces of furniture and other works of carpentry for friends and charity groups.

In the meantime, he tried to get over his defeat, which had plunged him and Rosalynn into sorrow and bitterness. He needed to rest and heal. He didn't get much chance, however. When he became president, Carter had asked his brother Billy to run the family businesses. Now, to his shock, Carter discovered that Billy had run up more than $1 million in debt. As the owner, Carter owed the money, but he didn't have it.

Because of his bad financial situation, Carter sold the agricultural conglomerate Archer Daniels Midland everything but his home and a few thousand acres of the old family farm. "To have lost that land would have been a devastating blow," he confessed.

Selling the business brought in some money, and his presidential pension gave him more, but he still didn't have enough to pay off his entire debt. Fortunately, publishers offered him and Rosalynn large sums of money to write memoirs. They accepted payment in advance and got down to work. Carter enjoyed writing *Keeping Faith*, his story of the White House years.

STEPPING OUT

Presidents traditionally wait months or even years before publicly criticizing their successors. Carter kept quiet only until May 18. "The United States government is pulling back from the so-called 'intervention' in

After losing the election, Carter and his family returned home to Plains.

matters of human rights. . . . [using] a critique of my own administration as having been naïve and excessively idealistic," he said in a speech to the New York Board of Rabbis, "[but] my policy—which certainly was not new—expressed the most profound yearnings and concerns of the American people." About Reagan's aggressive military policy, he said, "Further arming our country is not a substitute for mutually advantageous and properly balanced treaties." The speech made headlines nationwide.

Carter remained politically active while out of office. Anwar Sadat came to Plains. Carter enjoyed the visit, which proved that at least one major world leader still respected him. Later that month, Carter visited China at the invitation of the Chinese government. The Chinese received him with high honors, including a meeting with the prime minister, as if he were still president.

Then Sadat died. On October 6, he was witnessing a military parade when some soldiers broke ranks and opened fire at him. The soldiers

Jimmy Carter, the Author

Over the years, Carter has written numerous books ranging from his memoirs on his days in the White House to a children's book that his daughter Amy illustrated titled *The Little Baby Snoogle-Fleejer.*

belonged to Islamic Jihad, a militant organization that hated Sadat for making peace with Israel. His sudden death hurt Carter deeply.

As a sign of respect for Sadat, President Reagan asked all of the living former presidents to attend his funeral. Carter flew with Gerald Ford and Richard Nixon. While he didn't warm up to Nixon, Carter chatted with Ford about life both in the White House and afterwards. The conversation was the beginning of a close, warm, and unexpected friendship.

Four U.S. presidents, (from left to right) Ronald Reagan, Gerald Ford, Jimmy Carter, and Richard Nixon, traveled together to attend the funeral of Anwar Sadat.

ENTER THE CENTER

Carter had always worked toward goals. He had sought to enter the USNA, rise in the navy, and achieve success in business and politics. Now, although he was busy, he had no overriding goal to reach. Like other presidents, he was planning to create a library to house speeches and other documents from his presidency, but a mere building felt dead to him. He wanted something living.

One night in January of 1982, Rosalynn noticed that her husband couldn't sleep. He had always slept well, even amid the stress of international crises, so she asked if he felt sick. No, he answered: I know what to do with the library. We'll make it a place in which to resolve conflicts.

His inspiration came from the Camp David Accords, among other things. Carter wanted a permanent meeting place in which he could bring leaders together and help them patch their differences. It would handle other missions as well, such as improving international health care and education.

Carter spent the next several months planning the organization that he would call the Carter Center and asking his old political campaign donors for money to build and run it. He kept busy in other ways as well. In April 1982, he announced that he would teach government and related topics at Atlanta's Emory University. In June, when the Israeli military invaded Lebanon with the Reagan Administration's approval, he publicly criticized Reagan and the Israelis. In October, *Keeping Faith* hit bookstores, and he promoted it with interviews and public appearances. In March 1983, he visited the Middle East and forged a trusting relationship with Syrian president Hafiz al-Assad, even though Assad severely restricted his people's human rights, opposed the Camp David Accords, and supported Iran in its war with Iraq.

On September 26, 1983, Carter's sister Ruth died of pancreatic cancer, the disease that had taken their father's life. On October 30, the same illness killed their mother. Their deaths hit Carter hard. These personal losses didn't stop him from working, however. A week after his mother's death, Carter and Gerald Ford hosted the first Carter Center event, "Five Years After Camp David." Because the Carter Center had no buildings of its own yet, the conference took place at Emory University. From November 6 through 9, scholars, ambassadors, and foreign ministers from the United States and most Middle Eastern countries strolled the campus to talk peace and sometimes argue and shout about it. The conference proved that Carter still had the world's respect. He could attract powerful, stubborn, quick-tempered people and make them try to work together.

On the other hand, Carter's fellow Democrats avoided him. Presidential candidates usually want a former president to campaign for

The Carter Center

Today, the Carter Center in Atlanta remains committed to preventing and resolving conflicts, supporting human rights, and improving public health. The center employs more than one hundred people and is funded by private donations. The Jimmy Carter Library and Museum is housed in a building attached to the center.

them. As 1984's elections approached, though, Carter remained so unpopular among the American people that candidate Walter Mondale distanced himself. Carter understood why Mondale and other candidates behaved that way, but he didn't like it. Fortunately, he had other tasks to keep him busy.

BUILDING A HABITAT

In the late 1960s, a marketing executive from Alabama named Millard Fuller was in his early thirties, a millionaire, and miserable. His devotion to wealth was ruining his marriage and his belief in himself as a good person.

Fuller gave his riches away and dedicated his life to doing charity work. In 1976, after aiding ventures that set up communities for the poor, he founded Habitat for Humanity International.

Habitat builds houses for the underprivileged. Donors supply land and materials, or the money to buy them. The families who will own and live in the houses build them with the help of Habitat volunteers.

Since leaving office, Carter had supported Habitat with donations and speeches, but Fuller wanted more from Carter. Early in March 1984, the former president put on jeans and a work shirt and joined a Habitat crew that was building homes in Americus. The job married Carter's hobby of woodworking to his strong work ethic and Christian values, and he loved it. Later that year, he and Rosalynn rode a bus to New York City with a Habitat for Humanity work group and spent several days renovating a ramshackle tenement building into safe, affordable apartments.

The trip was the first of what Habitat for Humanity came to call Jimmy Carter Work Projects. Every year, the former president has spent at

Over the years, Carter has volunteered his time to work on numerous projects for Habitat for Humanity.

least one week at a Habitat site, pounding nails and breathing sawdust like any other volunteer.

AS ACTIVE AS EVER

By his sixtieth birthday on October 1, 1984, the man whom America had voted out of office was earning the world's admiration. That month, he spent a week and a half in South America, where he spoke out for human rights. He was working on *The Blood of Abraham*, a book about the Arab-Israeli conflict. He lectured and held seminars at Emory University and made furniture for friends and relatives.

He had hired a manager to run the Carter Center's day-to-day business, but he involved himself in most major decisions, from hiring employees to building the center's headquarters. He grew especially interested in the Center's "Closing the Gap: The Burden of Unnecessary Illness," a health-care conference held in late autumn of 1984.

Carter lived a fairly healthy life. Nevertheless, his family's history of cancer kept him alert for any signs of the disease. Neither he nor Rosalynn indulged much in fat, salt, or other unhealthy substances. He kept in shape by running. At age sixty-two, he even took up skiing.

GLOBAL 2000

As if he weren't busy enough, Carter took on a new responsibility. In a presidential speech delivered on May 23, 1977, Carter had promised "a one-year study of the probable changes in the world's population, natural resources, and environment through the end of the century." The State Department and another agency, the Council on Environmental Quality, got to work. *The Global 2000 Report to the President of the U.S.* warned, "The world in 2000 will be more crowded, more polluted, less stable ecologically, and more vulnerable to disruption than the world we live in now."

Carter remembered the report in 1985 after Ryoichi Sasakawa entered his life. The Japanese billionaire boat-builder aided a variety of charities, including the Carter Center. When a famine struck Ethiopia in 1983 and 1984, Sasakawa gave the United Nations a huge donation to help feed the starving people, but he wanted to do more. He organized a conference on world hunger to take place in Switzerland during July of 1985 and invited Carter.

The conference's reports of starvation, particularly in Africa, touched Carter deeply. Soon after the conference, he founded a new Carter Center program and named it Global 2000. It joined forces with the Sasakawa Africa Association, a group that Sasakawa created to help Africans get healthy food. The Global 2000/Sasakawa Africa Association set up its first office during June of 1986 in Accra, the capital of the African nation of Ghana.

One of Global 2000's first jobs was attacking worms. Guinea worms live in tiny fleas that swim in pools of stagnant water, mostly in Africa. When people drink the water and swallow the fleas, they also swallow young guinea worms, known as larvae. "Inside a human's abdomen, the larvae mature and grow, some as long as three feet," says the Carter Center's Web site. "After a year, the worm slowly emerges through an agonizingly painful blister in the skin."

Guinea worm infection can lead to deadly illnesses such as tetanus. During the 1980s, more than ten million people suffered from guinea worms, and another ninety million lived in conditions in which they were likely to become infected.

Carter heard about guinea worms in spring of 1986 from his friend Peter Bourne, a top health advisor during Carter's presidency. Bourne pointed out that simple equipment, such as water filters and purifiers, could eliminate guinea worms, but the areas that suffered most didn't have enough money or political power to get the equipment and train people to use it.

Working with groups such as the United Nations World Health Organization, Global 2000 attacked the problem. In 1986, more than three million people suffered from guinea worm infection. By 1994, the number had sunk to 100,000 and was still falling.

THE CENTER OPENS

For years, the Carter Center had struggled along without a home, using space at Emory University. On Carter's sixty-second birthday, the situation changed.

On October 1, 1986, after two years of construction, the Carter Center opened. Located on 37 acres (15 hectares) of hillside in Atlanta near Emory and Georgia Tech, the center's round, white buildings and green-lawned, woodsy campus were so beautiful that it became a popular spot to hold weddings.

In mid-November, the Carter Center hosted a conference that created a new tool to help Carter repair the world. Carter and Gerald Ford led a conference of political leaders and advisors called "Reinforcing Democracy in the Americas." Since the 1500s, faraway emperors and local tyrants had ruled most Latin American countries. In the twentieth century, though, some Latin nations were struggling to create democracies.

Battling Rosalynn

"We simply could not concur [agree]," Jimmy Carter wrote in 1996. "It soon became impossible for us to communicate directly, so we exchanged increasingly unpleasant comments through our word processors." He was talking about Rosalynn and the 1987 book that they wrote, a collection of advice on health and longevity called *Everything to Gain: Making the Most of the Rest of Your Life.*

"There was no possible way we could have worked in the same room. That would have been lethal," Carter told an interviewer. Fortunately, their editor stepped in as referee. From then on, they simply submitted separate sections. "It saved our marriage," Carter said. The arguments paid off. *Everything to Gain* became a national best seller.

Carter wanted the leaders at "Reinforcing Democracy" to help the new republics avoid unfair elections and power-hungry dictators.

With his fellow politicians, Carter formed the Council of Freely Elected Heads of Government. He would lead this team of more than a dozen current and former presidents, prime ministers, and others to promote democracy, peace, and international cooperation. As more nations held their first elections, Carter and other council members visited polling places to ensure that the voting process ran fairly.

PERSONAL LOSS AND PROFESSIONAL CHALLENGES

On September 26, 1988, Carter's brother Billy died of pancreatic cancer. The same illness took his sister Gloria on March 5, 1990.

Rather than dwell on his pain, Carter threw himself into his work. He disliked 1988's presidential election, which he called "the worst campaign

Carter lost two of his siblings to cancer in the late 1980s and early 1990s. Jimmy visits with his brother Billy, sisters Gloria and Ruth, and mother Lillian during happier times.

I've ever seen" because it involved "so much name-calling and mud-slinging." To help heal the nation, Carter and Gerald Ford created a non-partisan, book-length report called *American Agenda*, filled with policy advice for incoming president George H. W. Bush. Bush received the volume graciously but ignored its suggestions.

Carter had no better luck with elections in Panama a few months later. Since 1983, military chieftain Manuel Noriega had controlled the country. In May of 1989, Noriega held elections, but Carter and others expected him to rig them.

On May 5, Carter flew to Panama. He and his team of observers found Noriega's soldiers shutting down polling places and destroying ballots. He went to the building where Noriega's men were counting the votes and saw them altering ballots to make the count come out as Noriega wanted. In the room stood a raised platform or stage. Carter climbed onto it and demanded to know if the counters were "*honestos o ladrones*," which means "honest men or thieves." No one listened. That night, Carter angrily told the international press that the election was a fraud.

The world suddenly saw Carter as a fearless defender of democracy. Nothing seemed to stop him. In late July 1989, he visited Africa to convince government leaders to support Global 2000. For several days starting on September 7, he assembled the principal players of Ethiopia's long-running civil war at the Carter Center to negotiate peace. Beginning on September 16, he spent several days in Nicaragua to prepare the country to hold democratic elections.

As president in 1979, Carter had given Nicaraguan president Daniel Ortega aid money. In 1981, President Reagan cut off the funding and started supporting rebel forces called Contras, named after the Spanish word for "against." After attacks by Contras and protests from other Nicaraguans, Ortega cracked down on the citizens' rights and freedoms. The crackdown, plus an economic collapse, raised even more demands that Ortega change his ways. Under pressure, Ortega called an election for February 25, 1990.

On February 23, Carter went to Nicaragua with teams of observers to monitor the election. He liked Ortega and expected him to win. However, Ortega lost. On election night, with Rosalynn at his side, Carter gave Ortega the bad news. Ortega refused to accept it. Carter gently pressed him: "I can tell you from my own experience that losing is not the end of the world." "I thought it was the end of the world!" Rosalynn interrupted in a burst of good-humored honesty that helped loosen the tension in the room. Her husband went on, "Your greatest accomplishment as president will be if you lead a peaceful transition of power."

Ortega still didn't want to quit his job, but he did it. He became one of Central America's few leaders to give up power voluntarily. Secretary of State James Baker said, "I don't think that Ortega would have accepted the results in 1990 had President Carter not been down there."

MEETING ARAFAT

In a Paris hotel in April 1990, Carter fulfilled a long-time wish. He met Yasir Arafat. Born in Jerusalem, Arafat grew up wanting Palestinians to rule the State of Israel. In the late 1950s, he and fellow Palestinian Khalil el-Wazir founded Fatah, a code name for the Palestine National Liberation Movement. Fatah used violence in attempts to frighten Jews out of the region. Arafat joined the Palestine Liberation Organization in 1969 and turned it into the most effective of the groups seeking power for Palestinians. In December of 1988, the United Nations invited Arafat to speak before its General Assembly as a genuine head of state, even though the state had no land yet.

Carter, who had often stood up for Palestinian rights, wanted to meet Arafat, but conflicting schedules and concerns about safe places to meet had kept them apart. Finally, on April 4, they met.

They didn't agree on everything, but the two workaholics formed a bond. As time went on, Carter helped Arafat write speeches. When a plane carrying Arafat crashed in the Libyan desert during April 1992, Carter phoned the White House and asked for American spy satellites to find the plane.

Carter first met with Arafat in 1990. Later Carter visited Arafat in 1996 for the Palestinian elections.

Carter's friendship may have helped Arafat learn to trust Americans during peace talks with President Bill Clinton of the United States and Prime Minister Yitzhak Rabin of Israel. In any event, Clinton granted Carter a front-row seat at the White House in September 1993, when Arafat and Rabin signed a peace accord. The treaty gave Palestinians the right to govern themselves and installed Arafat as their national leader until they could hold elections.

The high point of Carter's relationship with Arafat may have come on January 20, 1996, Palestinian election day. Carter led a forty-person delegation to monitor the elections, which would name a ruling council and president. Arafat was running for the top job, and Carter spent the evening before the election with the candidate, his young wife, and their infant daughter.

Extremist Muslim groups opposed the elections, Israeli policemen who watched the polling places scared some Palestinians away from voting, and Arafat's Fatah Party apparently kept the names of opposing candidates off some ballots. Nevertheless, Palestinians turned out to vote in huge numbers, Carter decreed the elections fair and free, and Arafat won a gigantic 88.1 percent of the presidential vote.

WAR AND BOOKS

On August 1, 1990, Iraq's Saddam Hussein sent troops to invade the neighboring, oil-rich nation of Kuwait. Within a week, President Bush was gathering international support for an invasion of Iraq, which Carter publicly opposed. On November 20, Carter even asked the leaders of France, China, and the Soviet Union to block Bush's

invasion, a move that many Americans considered disloyal and unpa-
triotic.

By the time the invasion started in January 1991, Carter muted his
criticisms of Bush. Besides, other jobs were keeping him busy. In December
of 1990, he oversaw the first free national elections on the Caribbean
nation of Haiti. In April 1991, he went to China. In front of hundreds at
the Chinese Foreign Affairs College, which trains China's diplomats, he
criticized the government's policy of jailing protestors and called for
"amnesty to all non-violent dissidents." In June, he helped to build Habitat
for Humanity homes in Miami. When he wasn't traveling, he often taught
Sunday-school Bible classes at Plains' Maranatha Baptist Church.

He was also writing. Since leaving the White House, Carter had
published four books—five including 1984's *Negotiation: The Alternative
to Hostility*, a transcript of one of his speeches. Over the next decade,
he would write eight more books, revise and update three others for
new editions, and assemble an anthology of material that he'd written
years earlier.

Several of the books became instant best sellers. Some of them, such
as an explanation of his religious beliefs titled *Living Faith*, continued
selling strongly year after year. While other former presidents made for-
tunes by giving speeches or serving as directors of large corporations,
Carter said that his job title was "author."

THE ATLANTA PROJECT

In autumn 1991, Emory University president James Laney suggested
something that piled even more work onto Carter's plate. Laney had

helped him set up the Carter Center, but he wanted the international peacemaker to focus on local problems.

Inner-city residents of Atlanta and other urban areas endured poverty, unemployment, homelessness, and other crises. Carter felt guilty about hopping the globe to solve problems while neglecting his home state of Georgia. On October 25, he called for Atlanta's business and community leaders to help him improve the city. The crusade soon got named The Atlanta Project, or TAP.

In early 1992, one of TAP's first projects saw Carter and Rosalynn take about fifteen to twenty bright but troubled teenagers on a ski trip to Crested Butte, Colorado, where they hobnobbed with prominent TAP supporters. The trip seemed to help the teenagers so much that Carter turned it into an annual event.

As time passed, TAP divided the Atlanta area's worst neighborhoods into twenty "clusters." Carter asked each cluster's residents to identify their worst problems. To get the equipment and manpower to fix the problems, Carter recruited government agencies, ordinary citizens from outside the clusters, and Atlanta-based companies such as Coca-Cola and Delta Airlines.

Still, by the end of 1992, TAP seemed to be accomplishing nothing, possibly because Carter had encouraged Georgians to spread themselves out over a vast number of projects rather than work together on one at a time. Eventually, though, TAP made headway. In April of 1993, for instance, Carter led about 7,000 volunteers in going door-to-door and asking parents to bring their children to immunization centers. Within days, more than 15,000 children received shots to protect themselves against common childhood diseases.

Carter's involvement in TAP didn't keep him from other activities. He developed a passion for mountain climbing and often found himself near good climbing places in regions where he worked on other projects. In May 1993, he monitored elections in the South American nation of Paraguay. In November, he visited Sudan, a country near Egypt, to help calm a civil war. In 1994, he went to North Korea for his most dangerous job yet. He went there to head off a nuclear war.

CARTER IN KOREA

North Korea and South Korea had had a strained relationship for nearly fifty years. Both countries wanted to have nuclear bombs, a prospect that worried the U.S. government. After long negotiations, in 1991, the two Koreas signed a treaty renouncing nuclear weapons. In early 1994, though, the U.S. Central Intelligence Agency announced that North Korea was developing the forbidden armaments. President Bill Clinton considered invading the country and urged the United Nations to sanction, or pressure, North Korea by cutting it off from trade and financial aid. North Korean premier Kim Il-Sung answered, "Sanctions mean outright war."

"I had despised Kim Il-Sung for fifty years," Carter said in 2003. He blamed Kim for starting the Korean War. Now, though, Carter had a chance to prevent a new war. On June 12, 1994, he left for North Korea.

Before the first day of negotiations, he awoke at 3 A.M., a sign of worry for a sound sleeper like Carter. During the talks that day, he found Kim tough but open to preventing war.

Finally, at 12:30 A.M., Carter called the White House. He said that he was about to appear on the worldwide news channel CNN to announce that he and Kim had reached a deal. President Clinton was talking with top officials about invading. They turned on CNN, and there was Carter. He announced that Kim would stop developing nuclear weapons, would allow inspectors from the United Nations International Atomic Energy Agency to oversee his actions, and would negotiate with the United Nations to settle any conflicts. After further talks with Kim, Carter announced—wrongly, it turned out—that the United Nations wouldn't sanction North Korea.

Clinton was still pushing for sanctions and hated Carter's declaration that they would not put them into place. In Clinton's eyes, Carter had hijacked American foreign policy and made Clinton himself look useless. Moreover, many people in the Clinton Administration and the press felt that Kim wouldn't live up to his agreements and that Carter was foolish to trust him. Nevertheless, Carter had cooled a crisis and may have prevented a nuclear war.

OFF TO HAITI

Carter didn't take much time to rest before plunging into another conflict, this time in Haiti. The citizens of Haiti had elected young priest Jean-Bertrand Aristide as their president, but army general Raoul Cedras overthrew him and turned Haiti into a military dictatorship. On July 31, 1994, the United Nations passed Resolution 940, which authorized its member nations "to form a multi-national force . . . to facilitate [bring about] the departure from Haiti of the military leadership."

By September 13, a U.S. Navy invasion fleet was heading for Haiti, where Cedras and his troops were preparing to fight back. Americans and Haitians would kill each other unless someone could make Cedras resign.

Carter wanted the job and was pleased when President Clinton asked him to do it. Clinton sent retired general Colin Powell and Georgia senator Sam Nunn to accompany Carter and possibly to keep him from taking control as he had in Korea. On September 16, the three flew to Haiti.

They met with Cedras the next day to tell him that a bloodbath would occur unless he resigned. A turning point in the negotiations came the next day, when the threesome met Cedras's family. The dictator's son was celebrating his tenth birthday. Carter gave the boy a Carter Center pocketknife. The gift seemed to warm the family to Carter. He turned to the strong-willed Mrs. Cedras, who wielded great power over

Carter traveled to Haiti to help restore the elected president to office after a military leader overthrew him.

her husband. Though her striking beauty nearly mesmerized Carter, he told her that her husband's resigning to prevent an invasion would be the honorable thing to do.

On September 18, as battleships approached, Cedras agreed to leave power. American troops entered Haiti not to fight but to keep the people secure and peaceful until their democratically elected leader could return.

News headlines hailed Carter as a life-saving hero. It was a great way to approach his seventieth birthday on October 1.

GOING TO BOSNIA

Carter ended 1994 with yet another dangerous trip. This time he went to the Eastern European country of Bosnia.

In 1946, communist dictator Josip Broz Tito had pulled together several southeastern European states and ethnic groups to form the nation of Yugoslavia. After he died in 1980, the country slowly fragmented. In 1991, former Yugoslav states, such as Croatia, Slovenia, and Bosnia-Herzegovina, started declaring their independence. Within some of the new nations, an ethnic group called the Serbs wanted to govern themselves, but the national governments refused to let them. The Serbs fought back. Civil wars ripped the young countries apart.

By mid-December 1994, Bosnian Serb warlord Radovan Karadzic had sent Carter a message: come to Bosnia and negotiate a cease-fire. Carter accepted.

By going where bullets were flying, Carter risked his life. What's more, the Clinton Administration doubted that he could do much good.

Many experts considered Karadzic a war criminal who had ordered soldiers to kill innocent Bosnian civilians, including children, and to destroy Bosnian homes and businesses. In less than three days, however, Carter got the warring sides to agree to a four-month cease-fire.

BACK TO THE UNITED STATES

Carter spent the beginning of 1995 in the United States. He was promoting *Always a Reckoning*, a recently published book of his poetry, and taking The Atlanta Project nationwide. Leaders in other troubled cities had been contacting TAP's offices for advice. Carter and his staff turned the advice into the America Project, an organized program to help civic leaders create their own versions of TAP.

In March, Jimmy and Rosalynn went to see how Nigeria, Sudan, and other Africa nations were handling diseases such as guinea worm. A civil war in Sudan blocked doctors from finding and treating the sick. To give the doctors a chance, Carter negotiated a cease-fire that lasted for months.

As the 1990s rolled on, Carter continued trying to solve the world's problems. He wrote books and magazine and newspaper articles on world affairs, witnessed foreign elections, and taught at Emory University and Maranatha Baptist Bible College. He also gave interviews, some of which criticized U.S. foreign policy and angered the Clinton Administration.

During this period, Carter was apparently having the time of his life. In giving interviews for his best-selling book *The Virtues of Aging*, he even spoke happily about the close relationship that he and Rosalynn still shared.

He received honor after honor. In December 1998, the United Nations gave him its Human Rights Prize "for courage and determination in promoting and protecting human rights." In August 1999, President Clinton gave him the Presidential Medal of Freedom, the United States's highest civilian honor. The press honored his seventy-fifth birthday on October 1 with flattering articles and respectful interviews.

Carter seemed to be several places at once. Five days after his birthday, he visited Switzerland for the unveiling of a statue honoring the fight against the tropical disease river blindness, a cause that he had supported for years. October 16 saw him in the African nation of Mali to cheer on an organization that researched groundnut, a crop that might help end world hunger. In November, he monitored an election in Mozambique and spoke at Emory University about his 1994 trip to North Korea. In December, he negotiated a treaty between Uganda and Sudan; joined with Gerald Ford in asking television executives to give

The Carters received the Medal of Freedom from President Bill Clinton in 1999.

political candidates free broadcasts to discuss their views; and visited Panama to oversee the Panama Canal's final transfer from American to Panamanian control. Along the way, he kept up a vigorous exercise program and visited wealthy donors to raise money for the Carter Center. A biographer said in 2000, "He burns out Secret Service agents. They can't keep up with him."

VISITING CUBA

Though Carter enjoyed his success and popularity, he risked losing it in May 2002 when he went to Cuba. The island 90 miles (145 km) from Florida had troubled the United States for decades.

After revolutionary leader Fidel Castro took over in 1959, he formed a communist government that allied itself with the Soviet Union and opposed the United States. In the early 1990s, the Soviets had given up communism and stopped supporting Cuba, but the U.S. government and Castro still considered each other to be enemies. American law generally wouldn't let Americans visit Cuba or do business there.

As president, Carter had lightened some of the rules against dealing with the island. As an ex-president, he had worked with nations similar to Cuba. He wanted to go there. Castro, always ready to attract attention and support, wanted him to come. President George W. Bush opposed Castro and didn't want Carter to visit, but by mid-2002, Carter had built up so much prestige that Bush chose not to stop him.

Castro welcomed Carter by promising to let him go anywhere and talk to anyone, even anti-Castro rebels. The trip's peak came on May 14, when Carter gave a speech in Spanish over Cuban television. "Your constitution recognizes freedom of speech and association, but other laws deny these freedoms to those who disagree with the government." He went on to support a petition drive to let Cubans "change laws peacefully by a direct vote." For decades, no one in Cuba had spoken such words so freely and publicly.

Carter's five-day trip didn't change any of Bush's or Castro's policies. Many American conservatives hated the sight of Carter and Castro together and attacked Carter for apparently befriending another in a line of dictators and warlords from Daniel Ortega and the Shah of Iran to Kim Il Sung and Radovan Karadzic.

Nevertheless, Carter's visit stood as a landmark. It was the first trip to Cuba by a U.S. president in more than seventy years.

WINNING THE NOBEL PRIZE

After leaving Cuba, Carter kept to his typically busy schedule. He constructed Habitat for Humanity homes in South Africa, monitored elections in Venezuela, participated in Carter Center seminars and other events, and worked on writing a novel set during the American Revolution. Around 4:00 A.M. on October 11, the phone rang at his home in Plains. A Nobel Prize committee was calling from Oslo, Norway, to tell Carter that he had won the Nobel Peace Prize, the highest honor for any statesman or philanthropist. "I had a feeling of disbelief," Carter told reporters. "I am delighted, humbled, and very grateful."

Dignitaries around the world had been nominating Carter for the prize since 1978's Camp David negotiations. The committee gave it to him in 2002 partly as a slap at President Bush. The president was planning to invade Iraq despite opposition from an international peace movement and many world leaders, including Carter. Nobel committee

The Nobel Prize Committee recognized Carter in 2002 for his peace efforts.

chairman Gunnar Berge announced that he saw the prize as a "kick in the leg" at Bush.

At the award ceremony on December 10 in Oslo, Berge praised Carter "for his decades of untiring effort to find peaceful solutions to international conflicts." Carter, in turn, gave a speech in which he concluded, "We can choose to alleviate suffering. We can choose to work together for peace. We can make these changes—and we must."

BEYOND THE NOBEL PRIZE

After returning from Oslo, Carter went to Venezuela to help heal a political crisis, finished writing his novel, built Habitat for Humanity homes in Georgia and Alabama, and wrote articles on topics from the war in Iraq to a revived nuclear-weapons program in North Korea to political strife in the African nation of Liberia. In the election year of 2004, Democratic presidential candidates no longer shunned him but actively sought his endorsement. As he approached his eightieth birthday that year, Carter continued to speak out for human rights and other causes close to his heart.

The man from Plains had lived a life that no one could have predicted. He was a successful politician who hated conventional politics, a military man who preached peace, and a champion of human rights who embraced dictators. His ready grin hid a capacity for grim fury, and his Christian humility clashed with a steely confidence. He was a country boy who became a sophisticated operator in international relations. He was a loser and a hero. He was a president and a peacemaker.

Timeline

1924 James Earl Carter, Jr., known as Jimmy, is born in Plains, Georgia, on October 1.

1939 World War II begins.

1941 The United States enters World War II.

1943 Carter leaves Georgia for the United States Naval Academy in Annapolis, Maryland.

1945 World War II ends.

1946 Carter graduates from USNA on June 5.

Carter marries Rosalynn Smith on July 7.

1952 Carter joins Admiral Hyman Rickover's team at the United States Atomic Energy Commission's Division of Reactor Development and Technology on October 16 to develop nuclear submarines.

1953 Carter's father dies on July 22. Carter quits the navy, returns to Plains, and takes over his father's businesses.

1954 The Supreme Court rules in *Brown* v. *Board of Education* on May 17, declaring school segregation to be illegal.

1962 Carter runs for state senate and wins.

1966 Carter runs for governor and loses.

1967 Carter and Rosalynn's daughter Amy is born on October 19.

1970 Carter runs for governor again and wins the election on November 3.

1971 Carter shocks Georgia when he says, "The time for racial discrimination is over" during his inaugural address on January 12.

1974 Carter announces his candidacy for president at the National Press Club on December 12.

1976 Carter wins the presidential election on November 2.

1977 Carter takes the presidential oath of office on January 20. Carter signs Panama Canal treaties on September 7.

1978 Senate approves Panama Canal treaties on April 18. Carter meets with Egypt's Anwar Sadat and Israel's Menachem Begin for peace talks at Camp David starting on September 5. They announce "A Framework for Peace in the Middle East" on September 17. Carter announces on December 15 that the United States will officially recognize China's communist regime as the legal government.

Congress passes a key Carter energy bill on October 15, creating the Department of Energy.

1979 Carter and Soviet leader Leonid Brezhnev sign the second Strategic Arms Limitation Talks treaty (SALT II) on June 18. Carter holds a domestic summit at Camp David starting on July 3.

The shah of Iran, a controversial American ally, flees his country and leaves Muslim fundamentalists in charge. Muslim fundamentalists overrun the U.S. embassy in Tehran, Iran, and take the occupants hostage on November 4. The Soviet Union invades Afghanistan on December 25.

1980 Carter loses his run for reelection to Ronald Reagan on November 4.

A military mission to rescue the hostages fails and kills eight servicemen on April 24. Iraq invades Iran on September 22.

1981 On January 19, Carter makes a deal with Iran to release the hostages.

Carter leaves office on January 20.

1982 Carter starts planning the Carter Center in January.

In April, Carter announces that he will teach government and related topics at Atlanta's Emory University.

Carter builds homes with Habitat for Humanity in early March; he will continue building homes with Habitat every year thereafter.

1985 Carter founds the health and hunger project Global 2000.

1986 The Carter Center opens on October 1.

Carter and others form the Council of Freely Elected Heads of Government in November.

1989 Carter makes international headlines by denouncing Panama's national elections in early May.

1990 Carter oversees Nicaraguan elections and eases President Daniel Ortega out of office voluntarily on February 25. Carter meets and befriends Palestinian leader Yasir Arafat on April 4. On November 20, Carter asks heads of foreign countries to oppose the United States's upcoming invasion of Iraq.

1991 On October 25, Carter announces the creation of The Atlanta Project.

1994 Carter heads off a possible nuclear war between the Koreas in June.

Carter persuades Haitian military dictator Raoul Cedras to resign, heading off a U.S. invasion, on September 18.

Carter negotiates a cease-fire in a Bosnian civil war in December.

1996 Carter supervises the first national Palestinian elections on January 20.

2002 Carter visits Cuba in mid-May as the first president to visit the island in more than seventy years.

Carter wins the Nobel Peace Prize on October 11.

To Find Out More

BOOKS

Carter, Jimmy. *An Hour Before Daylight: Memories of a Rural Boyhood*. New York: Simon & Schuster, 2001.

Carter, Jimmy. *Keeping Faith: Memoirs of a President*. New York: Bantam Books, 1982.

Carter, Jimmy. *Living Faith*. New York: Times Books, 1996.

Carter, Jimmy. *Turning Point: A Candidate, a State, and a Nation Come of Age*. New York: Times Books, 1992.

ORGANIZATIONS AND ONLINE SITES

American Experience: Jimmy Carter
http://www.pbs.org/wgbh/amex/carter/index.html

This Web site offers visitors information from the *American Experience* program on Jimmy Carter as well as timelines and additional resources.

The Carter Center
One Copenhill
453 Freedom Parkway
Atlanta, GA 30307
http://www.cartercenter.org

The Carter Center seeks to prevent and resolve conflicts, enhance freedom and democracy, and improve health worldwide.

Emory University
Atlanta, Georgia 30322
http://www.emory.edu

Emory has a number of connections with Carter and the Carter Center. Carter himself is an Emory professor.

Jimmy Carter Library and Museum
441 Freedom Parkway
Atlanta, Georgia 30307-1498
http://www.jimmycarterlibrary.org

The Jimmy Carter Library and Museum has photographs, documents, and displays that chronicle the Carter presidency and Jimmy Carter's life.

Jimmy Carter National Historic Site
300 North Bond Street
Plains, GA 31780
http://www.nps.gov/jica/

This area includes President Carter's residence, boyhood farm, school, and the railroad depot, which served as his campaign headquarters during the 1976 election.

The White House
http://www.whitehouse.gov

Learn more about Jimmy Carter and other past and present presidents.

A Note on Sources

Too much information is a problem in writing a biography of a modern president. When every major newspaper, magazine, and news broadcast covers a man's activities for more than thirty years, simply plowing through all of the reports, editorials, opinion columns, speeches, photos, and other documents is impossible. A presidential biographer's job isn't just to find information but to select the best of it.

A friend of Carter's, Peter Bourne, has written one of the finest general biographies of the man, *Jimmy Carter: A Comprehensive Biography from Plains to Post-Presidency*. The best book on Carter's life before he became president is probably *Dasher: The Roots and the Rising of Jimmy Carter* by *New York Times* White House correspondent James Wooten, who followed Carter on the 1976 campaign trail and got to know the man, his family, and his world. For the years after the presidency, University of New Orleans history professor Douglas Brinkley provided a superb account in *The Unfinished Presidency: Jimmy Carter's Journey Beyond the White House*. For facts of all kinds, I turned to the *Collier's Encyclopedia*, the *Grolier Encyclopedia of Knowledge*, and the *Encyclopaedia Britannica*.

Carter himself has written more books than probably any other president. The volumes that touch on his life story were uniquely valuable.

An Hour Before Daylight: Memories of a Rural Boyhood covers his early life; *Turning Point: A Candidate, a State, and a Nation Come of Age* discusses his first political campaign; *Keeping Faith: Memories of a President* delves into the White House years; and *Living Faith* spans his entire life to discuss his religious beliefs.

Television has provided a number of Carter interviews and profiles. The Public Broadcasting Service has delivered two shows in particular that proved immensely helpful. PBS's ongoing *NewsHour* has produced several superb interviews with Carter and reports and commentary on his life. *American Experience* produced a mini-series on Carter that covered his entire life and included interviews with a number of the people who knew him best.

The Internet is a superb source of information. The search engines Google and Alltheweb helped me dig up facts on every aspect of Carter's life. The Jimmy Carter Library and Museum in particular has an exceptional site. Carter's childhood gets an excellent treatment in the Web pages of the National Park Service's Jimmy Carter National Historic Site. The Web sites of the Carter Center and Emory University offer great storehouses of information on Carter's life after the presidency.

Many newspaper and magazine reporters have written about Carter over the years. To find newspaper and magazine articles, I consulted the databases LexisNexis, Infotrac, ProQuest, the Wilson Current Biography Database, and the Gale Group's Biography Resource Center Database. The online services of the Beverly Hills Public Library and Los Angeles Public Library helped immensely by providing many of these services.

Finally, I have paid visits to Atlanta, which helped me capture the feeling of Carter's life in that city.

—*David Seidman*

Index

About the Author

David Seidman is the author of more than twenty books, including *Cesar Chavez: Labor Leader*, *Secret Service Agents*, *Civil Rights*, *The Young Zillionaire's Guide to Supply and Demand*, *Secret Agent!*, *Exploring Careers in Journalism*, *All Gone: Things That Aren't There Anymore*, *U.S. Warplanes: F/A-18C Hornet*, and *Wonders of the World*.